SOLOMON'S SECRET

Solomon's Secret

A Commentary
on the
Song of Solomon

C. R. Oliver

SOLOMON'S SECRET

A COMMENTARY ON THE SONG OF SOLOMON

DR. C. R. OLIVER

P.O. Box 971
MONTGOMERY, TEXAS 77356
Email: croliver@sat.net

© 1999 C.R. Oliver

ISBN - 0-931221-08-0

**Ransom Press International
Bonita Springs, Florida**

Printed in Colombia

Table of Contents

Chapter 1	**A DRAMATIC PRODUCTION**	7
Chapter 2	**THE DRAMA IN SOLOMON'S SONG**	15
Chapter 3	**A HOLY KISS**	27
Chapter 4	**HOW IT ALL BEGAN**	47
Chapter 5	**THE BANQUET HALL**	67
Chapter 6	**PRECIOUS PRESENCE**	87
Chapter 7	**GOING TO THE GARDEN**	99
Chapter 8	**TORN VEIL AND STEADFAST HEART**	131
Chapter 9	**HE IS NEVER FAR AWAY**	151
Chapter 10	**THE PRINCE'S DAUGHTER**	163
Chapter 11	**THE SEALED HEART**	183

"All the Kethubin are indeed a holy thing, but the Song of Songs is a Holy of Holies."

"Origen, who is called the Father of Christian exegesis, enumerates the chief songs of the Bible and then says 'and after thou hast passed through all these thou must mount higher to sing with the Bridegroom the SONG OF SONGS.'"

(EXCERPTS FROM A PRIVATE COLLECTION, Rosenberg Library Rare Books Division, Galveston Island, Texas)
<u>Song of Solomon</u>, Elbert Hubbard, London: Roycroft Press, 1895

CHAPTER ONE

A DRAMATIC PRODUCTION

"The song of songs, which is Solomon's (Song 1:1,KJV)"

INTRODUCTION TO THE SONG

You are about to embark on the most intriguing adventure in your research of the Bible. I am able to say this because I have spent over twenty years searching the Song's pages and loving its message.

Song of Solomon is just what it says; it is Solomon's own song. It is a prophetic work and a personal tribute. He tells a story that on the surface appears to be simply a statement of love between a Shepherd Boy and a Shulamite girl. Because he was a man of tremendous intellect and wisdom, he uses the medium of a story to offer to God his own heart. This Song, which belongs to Solomon, will be one among millions of Songs, both written and to be written. Every believer will have his own version as his own life unfolds and enfolds with the life of Jesus.

In heaven, Revelation states there will be a new song sung to the Lamb. That song may be a combined chorus of identical words and phrases, or one penned by each believer. However it is to be sung, it will be a song of the Bride to the Bridegroom. It will be personal. It will be filled with meaning that only the two who have been made "one" will understand. This song will reflect the experiences of grace and love known only to them both. Jesus and His bride will sing to each other. Unique as it may sound, this book houses just such a song. It is a song from the bride to her lover and from her lover to her. It is a dialogue.

In my initial treatments of the Song, I used a transliterative narrative to familiarize audiences in Brazil and the United States with its content. I did this because of the difficulty in reading eight chapters of text and then taking time to preach from those eight chapters. I often instructed the persons attending to grant me license in approaching the book since it uses a dramatic format. In similar manner, in Chapter two of this text, I will give a general review of the Song of Solomon using story form to set its picture in the reader's mind.

While approaching the next chapter, a few basic concepts must be reviewed. The first is the type of text we are perusing. I call it a "stand alone book." This judgment is based on several similar cases in the Bible. The book of Job is one such case in point. Job is generally understood to be one of the first, if not the first book in the Bible. Its message is universal. Although it is the account of one man's life events, it has application to every person who lives a righteous life. Job is a classic example of a "stand alone" book because it is unlike other texts in the Bible. It must be treated differently than say, Deuteronomy. In the same way, the Song is both unique and universal. It tells the story of love which grows between two people who begin as strangers and through due process become "one."

Just as there are books that stand alone, there are special chapters within scripture that are complete within themselves; thus, they too "stand alone." Such a chapter is Revelation 12. Here, the writer stops the action of time and relates an account that begins with the birth of Christ and ends with eternity. Song of Solomon does the same. It begins with a personal encounter with the Lord and ends with the marriage of the Lamb, all within eight chapters.

My reference to Revelation is not without purpose. The Song of Solomon and the book of Revelation are books meant to be read and understood together. This comprises my second important thesis regarding my study of this text. These two books are paired in their treatment of the bride of Christ, the marriage of the Lamb, and the great marriage feast. They relate to one another and complement each other. Hopefully, you will agree once you have finished this book. For now, look at the final passages of both the Song and Revelation.

The last phrase in Revelation is also the last phrase of the Song. Isn't it extraordinary that in Revelation it is "the Spirit <u>and</u> the Bride" who bid the reader to drink of the water of life freely? Where Revelation reveals the completed bride in glory and honor, the Song of Solomon shows the development of the bride. Song of Solomon is the "A" to Revelation's "B." The Song begins with a Shulamite girl who is both unlearned and uncoiffured. She develops through many experiences into the magnificent compliment to her lover. I will show you in the Song where the Holy Spirit moves upon the life of the Shulamite and transforms her until she has the same nature as Jesus. Do not be shocked at the grace of equality, for it is imputed to the Bride similarly to righteousness. If this shocks you, think of what it did to my theology when the Spirit led me to understand this plan of the ages! Discovering this truth opened doors to other mysteries of the Bible which led to this twenty year venture. I find the Song to be the answer to many of the mysteries of the New Testament. Paul in Philippians 3:10ff says:

> "For my determined purpose is that I may know him – that I may progressively become more deeply and *intimately* acquainted with Him, perceiving and recognizing and understanding the *wonders of His Person,* more strongly and more clearly. And that I may in that same way come to know the power outflowing from His resurrection (which it exerts over believers);.... but I press on to lay hold of (grasp) and make my own, that which Christ Jesus, the Messiah, *has laid hold on me and made me His own."*
>
> (Amplified Version)

Is Paul saying that after preaching to most of the known world, writing the greater portion of the New Testament, and having experienced the Damascus road, he does not know Jesus to the degree he wants? Doesn't he possess the honor of knowing Jesus more intimately and deeply than any man on earth who lived after Jesus' ascension? Here enters the Song. Paul is speaking about knowing Jesus on the same level the Song speaks of knowing Him. He is calling into his life an intimacy that approximates the intimacy of lovers. Since nothing is more intimate in this world's relationships than the fellowship of lovers, Paul longs to have just such a relationship. Lovers who experience pillow talk, the lying down and rising up talk, the eating around the same table talk, are the love relationship he longs for. Lovers tend to bond during sessions of talking with one another every day. In overcoming the trials of life, their intimacy takes on a character known only to them. The lovers in the Song are real lovers, the kind that Paul longs to be with Jesus. The Song is the story of two lovers: Jesus and you. This is what the Song of Solomon is about. From its pages, the believer will enter into the sacred secrets of two lovers committed to a life together. You (all who are the true Bride) and Jesus are those lovers!

The Pauline passage also speaks of mutual claim. The last phrase calls vivid attention to the greatest of all spiritual facts: that we press to lay hold on Him in the same way He has laid hold of us. Before you finish the Song, it will become evident that the Bride has claim to Him, just as He does to her. Allow me to show why I know this is true. There is a passage in Paul's writing that can only be understood in the terms of the Song. It is Ephesians 1:9-10:

> "Making known to us the mystery (secret) of His will – of His plan, of His purpose. (And it is this:) In accordance with His good pleasure (His merciful intention) which He had previously purposed and set forth in Him, (He planned) for the maturity of the times and the climax of the ages to unify all things and head them up and consummate them in Christ, (both) things in heaven and things on the earth.
> (Amplified Version)

Pay special attention to the word "mystery (secret)" and the word "consummate" (Amplified Version). I firmly believe that Solomon, with special wisdom from God, was privileged to fathom one of the greatest spiritual mysteries in the Bible. He saw through spiritual eyes how believers can encounter Jesus, fall in love with him, and ultimately become his Bride. For this reason, the Song is one of the most cherished books of the Bible.

Cherished is a good term at this point. To many who have tapped its pages, the Song has been little more than a proof text for marriage counseling or a quick reference using some of its beautiful passages to prove some distant point. Ask yourself to recall any pulpit which took the Song as it prime text and preached its entirety. More than likely if the text has been used in a church, it has been a text for a conference or a convention and not a text for pulpiteers. Because of this fact, I have asked a range of clergy their interpretation of the book. Their replies were sobering based on my knowledge of its sublime teaching.

Many wondered why it was kept in the Bible. Some related they could not use the text because of its subject matter. A Rabbi disclosed he had taught the book but did not comprehend its meaning. Some Protestant clergy confessed they had not used one line from its pages. Does this tell us something? Is not this a preserved word from God?

Because he wrote, "the fear of the Lord is the beginning of wisdom: and the knowledge of the holy is understanding (Prov. 9:10)," couldn't it be concluded that Solomon was capable of writing such a masterpiece? This masterpiece is now being drawn, by the Holy Spirit, into its proper place in Biblical study for the last days! Neglected through centuries, cast into minority position by clergy, even denounced by many, it has arrived "on time" and with glory. The very clothing by which it has been obscured enhances its beauty. Having chosen the dramatic form, Solomon utilizes the double entendre for his method of obscuring his revelation. He did not intend for the reader to apprehend its true meaning without enlightened understanding by the Holy Spirit. "He that hath ears to hear, let him hear what the Spirit says to the churches" is relevant in the Song.

Because of this premise, the reader must be aware of the method Solomon used in portraying his insights. When I refer to the double entendre, I mean there is a surface story with an underlying meaning. In other words, he used an allegory about two lovers while underlying their every action with a deeper message. We could surmise that Solomon[1] was writing a "How To" book. In telling how the Shulamite[2] became the bride of the Shepherd Boy, He also tells how a believer becomes the Bride of Jesus. Each message relates directly to becoming the Bride of Christ. The dramatic form was used to conceal its deeper message yet act as a vehicle of understanding for its intended subject: "the Bride." Because the Bride appears complete at the end of the ages, this makes the Song an end-time book. It is a play produced by God for the believer to view and thereby be taught.

---

[1]Solomon means "peace offering" in type and shadow of Jesus who would come later as the "Lamb of God".

[2]Shulamite means "the perfect one" in type and shadow of a future many membered bride without "spot or wrinkle" to be prepared for the Lamb.

Imagine viewing a dramatic production in which, before it ends, you recognize one of the lead characters is actually you. What awesome portent is that reality! The play is about you. What you have just seen in that production is a portrayal of events that had happened to you, were happening to you, and would be happening to you. Somehow, you are aware of having just reviewed the happiest ending imaginable to your life, and yet you have not gotten to the end of your life in time. This is the way we learn from the Song! The Song reveals how a believer becomes the Bride of Jesus. When I saw this truth, joy, praise, and the deepest love for Jesus that I had ever experienced overcame me. Solomon penned a masterpiece about the Bride of Jesus, and it has been preserved through the ages until the end-time when it has blossomed in its due season. He planted a flower which took almost three thousand years to bloom, but it is "on time." Its fragrance now fills the air!

As I said before, Solomon uses the dramatic form in writing his book. The Song becomes a unique art form all its own. How different it is from Ecclesiastes and Proverbs. Solomon uses a format not used in any other Biblical text. In his other works, Solomon uses didacticism; he philosophizes and teaches. This book utilizes combinations of words, sounds, light, human passion, and human situation to draw the reader-audience into its realm. Players upon the stage are only two: Solomon and the Shulamite. A chorus known as the daughters of Jerusalem surrounds the stage action. Their responsibility is to offer comment, keep the audiences' attention focused, and make appropriate responses to rhetorical questioning.

The Shulamite girl and the Shepherd Boy interact through scene sequences leading to a dramatic close in chapter eight. We see them fall in love and begin a progression to the time where they blend in every aspect of their lives. Solomon's use of poetry in motion and verbiage is both precise and meaningful. Dramatic timing is correct. The audience is invited into the most intimate of detail and dialogue. When finished, silent reflection takes the reader into the tent of "knowing." It is as if before the play, one's understanding was fragmented, and afterward there is sublime completeness. Once you "looked through a glass darkly," but now you are face to face with Jesus. You are now able to begin writing your personal "Song." (There comes a freedom to write your own song with candor and without inhibition once you fathom the Song.) Suddenly it is not improper to speak to Him about the most intimate of life's struggles. Our theology does not hinder us now. Outdated concepts of what is proper and what is not are swallowed up in blurting out our love for Him. His acceptance of our mortality is no longer a debate. We are held in His arms; we hear His words spoken in softness into our ears; we look into His eyes; we know that we have come to the place God wants us to be. Words will not be needed to express ourselves. (I believe that the silence spoken of in Revelation will be when the Bride looks upon Him and He the Bride. She knows He chose her as much as she chose Him! They are finally together forever.)

At last, the Bride reigns with him! Like the bride who stands beside a King, she stands in his glory. It is immaterial what her former social class has been, for her parentage is irrelevant. Her past is not a matter for discussion in the court of the King. Her authority derives from Him. Her status is by association. She has her own power in the kingdom like the Biblical Esther. Love has overcome, surpassed, encompassed and triumphed over every detail of life. She now stands coequal with Him, because He declares it so. What she has learned, what knowledge she possesses has come from Him. She reigns because the many days of contemplation, re-arranging, re-adjusting and revising her own attitude and self-concepts are over.

The marriage of the Lamb to a spotless Bride is the consummation of the agony and ecstasy of her own struggle alongside Him. Each of her steps forward is a journey into new awareness of her place in Him. The Song of Solomon is a portrayal of that journey. At last she stands beside Him, the culmination of a life built upon His promises. A living testament, without thought of being cast away, forgotten, or declared unacceptable, is this second Eve! Grafted into an eternal family and sanctioned by the Heavenly Father, she stands radiantly. Her future is secure. Wealth beyond measure belongs to both of them. By marriage she is a joint heir with Him. She is not an object; she is not a possession. She is the product of a mutual commitment. He is not whole without her, just as Adam was not whole without Eve. What He loves, she loves. What

He despises, she despises. What is said against her, done against her is said and done against Him. They are one!

As you enter the study of Solomon's Song, look at the changing identity of the Shulamite. She changes from self-deprecation, when she describes herself in Chapter one, to a person with self-assurance in Chapter eight. Like the heavenly bride of Revelation, she is changed from a person interested in her own world to a woman invested in their combined universe. In abandoning her world for His, she becomes His Eternal Companion.

CHAPTER TWO

THE DRAMA IN SOLOMON'S SONG

"Let Him kiss me with kisses of His mouth:...(Song 1:2, KJV)"[1]

AN ALLEGORY OF LOVE

Let us enter Solomon's theater and experience his beautiful work. It will be fitting to review each scene from a director's point of view. In that way you, as the reader, will capture the progression and know something of the inner workings of the play. It will be necessary to read all the Song of Solomon in one setting and then continue to view the scenes with that knowledge. After this chapter, which familiarizes the reader with the book as a whole, the subsequent chapters will detail verses as they appear in sequence. Beginning with chapter one, the method of discovery will be a brief synopsis of the setting, followed by a review of the text. Now look at Chapter One, scene one of the <u>Song of Solomon</u>.

SCENE I:

The Shulamite woman reflects (in a place of solitude) about her love for a Shepherd-King. Her reflections are verbal. She sets the stage for a flashback to her earliest days as a shepherd girl on the Judean Hills. She reminisces from the point of view of a grown and experienced woman, then flashes back to her unlearned beginning.

> "Let him kiss me with the kisses of his mouth: for thy love is better than wine. Because of the savour of thy good ointments thy name is as ointment poured forth, therefore do the virgins love thee. Draw me, we will run after thee: the king hath brought me into his chambers: we will be glad and rejoice in thee, we will remember thy love more than wine: the upright love thee."
>
> (Song 1:2-4 KJV)

---

[1]"Kisses of His mouth:" The Word poured forth to man by Jesus is like kisses covering all of mankind.

Note the uncharacteristic beginning for such a production. The girl cries out for her lover to kiss her. In the first four verses, she calls the audience to an intimacy rarely viewed in the ancient world but highly appropriate for our generation. She then begins weaving her story of love, beginning with its humble start. She remembers vividly how it all began.

A lonely shepherd girl sits watching her flock on a deserted Judean hillside. It is midday, and she is lamenting that her skin is sunburned and parched from the hot sun. Her anger turns to her brothers who have determined her fate by assigning her this task. It would seem that her father has died, so she and her mother are left in the hands of the eldest son for care. To divide the labor, her lot fell to tending goats (1:6-8). She assesses herself as being "comely," and one might conclude she is contemplating her marketability for attraction and marriage.

Rhetorically, the Shulamite appeals to the "daughters of Jerusalem" to make judgment as to the truth of her rationale.

> "O ye daughters of Jerusalem, as the tents of Kedar, as the curtains of Solomon. Look not upon me, because I am black, because the sun hath looked upon me: my mother's children were angry with me; they made me the keeper of the vineyards; but mine own vineyard have I not kept."
>
> (1:5-6 KJV)

The daughters of Jerusalem perform the duties of a chorus in this ancient play. They interact with the actors from time to time. Sometimes they will agree with the players, similar to saying "amen" to a minister's sermon; sometimes they will ask questions on their own, evoking a response from the players. Often they will move the action of the play into a different direction or focus. They arbitrate the scene changes. They change the focus between actors and give clarity to what is said or done. Many times they will remain silent and in so doing, give consent. Their place is unique in Biblical literature but not unlike the Angel of Heaven who escorts John from place to place. Also in Revelation 12, there is a similar action to that of the Song. Revelation 12 uses a flashback and flash-forward method to unveil its truth. This method offers clarity and reason to the scenes taking place in front of the observer. In like manner, the daughters of Jerusalem become interpreters for the observer. They may interject a thought or evoke a response, but in the end their job is to act on behalf of the audience (who would ordinarily not be ejaculatory during the play). Whether they encourage or remain silent, whether they comment affirmatively or challenge aggressively, they are a vital part of the action. It is necessary to separate their part from that of the Shulamite (bride) and her bridegroom (the Shepherd Boy who turns out to be King) for clarity's sake.

It is not long before the Shulamite's attention is drawn from her loneliness to the Shepherd Boy. Her soliloquy is broken by the approach of a distant figure leading his flock toward her. We are not told if they have met before; we can only assume, by her remarks to Him, they have. She wants to know the location for watering His sheep during the midday. Her inquiry is spiced with a comment about "loving him with her soul." We are not told whether this is verbalized or spoken under her breath. We do not know whether this is a thought that runs through her mind or whether it is a remark directed to the Shepherd. We do know she is telling the truth. She wants to be with Him; she does not just want protection from the other men present. She is interested in a closer relationship with Him. Otherwise, she would have been content to walk along with His companions and just be one of the group. In chapter 8, she will use the knowledge gleaned from His companions to couch her closing appeal. She does not hesitate in stating her desire:

> "Tell me, O thou whom my soul loveth, where thou feedest, where thou makest thy flock to rest at noon: for why should I be as one that turneth aside by the flocks of thy companions?"
>
> (Song 1:7, KJV)

The shepherd girl's aggressive behavior may or may not be uncommon in her period of history, but of this we are aware, it is portrayed for a purpose. She is a peer to the Shepherd Boy and is well enough acquainted with Him to feel comfortable with it.

The daughters of Jerusalem inject their presence at this point. They ask the girl, in a teasing way, if she does not already know where the Shepherd feeds His flock? They intimate that she should follow the trail of the sheep. We are not sure why they do this, but more than likely they are setting the scene to cast the Shulamite as a naivete.

The girl is struggling with a poor self-concept and feeling very unattractive. She is sensitive to her low station in life compared to a Shepherd Boy, who evidently is destined for greater things. Because of His age, He is assigned temporarily to the task of the sheep. She is assigned to the goats because of an economical situation. Her flock is small, and she is aware His flock is large, and He has many servants attending with Him. She has no servants.

The Shepherd Boy is totally enamored of her. He can see nothing but the girl's beauty and speak only of her good points. He does not hear her comments about her lack. He is captured by her eyes, her smell, her purity. His words are meant to encourage, to engage, to solidify His heart with hers. He tells her of His home, which is like a mansion in her farthest dream. Her humble home has none of the splendor He describes. The terms He uses are polished, and His way with phrases captures the hour. He evidences a social and cultural background beyond hers. Their eyes meet, and somehow all these considerations fade. She acknowledges her love for Him (1:12-13) and invites His overtures.

SCENE II:

At this point, the scene changes; we are not told the interim. We do know that the scene changes to a banquet hall. We are not told what intervened, but a new stage of involvement is defined. This is not the same couple who cooed sweet love passages on a Judean Hill. (I could do as I did several times in my development of the understanding of the Song; I could interject my own scenario. My departure from the text is meant for clarification and in this brief area will not be based on scripture. Although it is conjecture, it makes the story flow with added ease.)

It occurs to me that the Shepherd Boy pledges His love to her and her to Him, then a turn of events causes Him to leave. I conjecture He is drawn from the menial task of sheep-care back to the Palace for greater duties. It is from this position of power that He calls for the Shulamite girl to be brought to Him.

I used to imagine that the girl was expectantly awaiting word from the Shepherd Boy as He had pledged to come for her. I also imagined the thoughts of her mind as she had faith in Him against the odds of doubt. How she must have defended Him against the reason of older brothers who surely sought to dissuade her. They must have told her that men always leave with a promise and never return. Probably her own mother sought to change her mind toward Him (as a hopeless cause) given the miles, the time, and the social distance. I imagined her lonely nights of remembering and the constant rehearsal of His words of love in her darkness.

All this imagining may or may not have been the case, but somehow through time, the shepherd girl knew one day the Shepherd Boy would honor His word. I can imagine an entourage from the King summoning her to the Palace. Whether she knew of His royalty at the time of their first love is of no consequence. However, her heart was pledged to the Shepherd boy. Imagine as she is brought into the Palace and told that she will be the bride of the King. Not knowing the Shepherd Boy was the King may have caused thoughts of betrayal to come to her mind. She is pledged to a Shepherd Boy on a Judean Hill, not the King. Marrying the King and not the Boy she fell in love with would be devastating. She finds herself caught in a dilemma. Can she love someone whom she has not met? Can she be happy with the King, while still being in love with the Shepherd Boy?

That the shepherd girl is in the King's Palace awaiting the person of the King is enough to conjure fear. (Upon entering the palace, more than likely she was tutored in social graces anticipating her new role. Included in her preparation would be a new coiffure, new garments and instructions how to wear them. She probably was instructed as to the likes and dislikes of the King. She was transformed from a Shepherd girl to a woman of court). Like Esther, she is enabled by God to assume the position of queen and consort to the King. She knows the rules and regulations. Her person in the mirror has changed both in mental imagery and physical appearance. She is beautiful!

Scene II takes place in a banquet hall. Filled with exotic foods and flowers, set with utmost care in detail, the table is a pleasure to all the girl's senses. She perhaps has never experienced such abundance as is now hers to possess. Sitting awaiting the arrival of the King, anticipation and perhaps unease surround her. The banquet room houses enough food for an army but is set for two.

The scene opens with a Solomonaic speech of grandeur. "I AM the rose of Sharon and the lily of the valleys (2:1, KJV)." Familiar passages escape His lips, and the shepherd girl sees Him enter the room. It is the Shepherd Boy! The King is the Shepherd Boy. Her elation is overrun by expressions of joy.

We hear the Shepherd-King's total words upon entering: "I am the rose of Sharon and the lily of the valleys. As the lily among thorns, so is my love among the daughters (2:1-2, KJV)." We see the shepherd girl's heart leap within her. She cries out, "As the apple tree is among the wood, so is my beloved among the sons. I sat down under his shadow with great delight, and his fruit was sweet to my taste (Song 2:3,KJV)." They enfold each other with love and the sweet phrases of love. Anyone would know that they are passionately in love with each other; they exclude all other matters from their focus.

The time for really knowing one another has come. The girl relaxes in the King's presence; they have no secrets, no untold pasts cloud their day. She feels rich by enjoying His riches. He tells her that all He has belongs to her and that the banquet is just a token symbol of the wealth available to her. How difficult it is for her to grasp her change from poverty, lack, and never having enough, to having anything she desires.

The couple embrace and make all the moves associated with loving another. Their words are soft and caring. Their manner is open and unevasive. To her He has pledged His kingdom, for He has found His kingdom in her. However, He is still King, and He has His duties. He leaves her presence. (In the next verse she is welcoming His return but that return is conditioned.)

The King returns but maintains a distance as He calls for the Shulamite to join Him. Although she wishes Him to remain with her in the banquet house where it is comfortable, she hears the first invitation in the Song for her to accompany Him. She would rather stay in the banquet hall and get acquainted with her new surroundings than to accept his offer. She would rather fill her time relaxing in the large rooms, getting acquainted with all that goes on there, than accompany Him on some journey to the streets. She has had enough of labor and other people. She can remember the hard times related to being among the populace and the fears that those events evoked. "No, let me stay here," is her supposed reply. He cautions her that doubts may arise in her heart if she spends too much time away from Him, yet He honors her will.

SCENE III:

Housed in her bedchamber, the Shulamite begins to ache for the Shepherd-King's presence. She leaves the chamber and goes into the streets in search of Him. The street is empty except for the night watch.

The girl is speaking to her inner being as she says, "I will arise now, and go about the city in the streets, and in the broad ways I will seek him whom my soul loveth: I sought him, but I found him not (3:2,KJV)." The King had requested her presence with Him, but she did not go. Now she is repenting. Her mind races with thoughts of Him. She encounters a watchman in the night. She inquires of the watchman if He has seen her love. He evidently has seen Him but does not know where He is presently. She leaves the watchman and shortly afterward meets her precious King. She embraces Him, kisses Him, and brings Him home with her. She wants Him to dwell in her mother's home as an acknowledgment of their betrothal. (Remember that betrothal in those days was tantamount to marriage. Joseph was betrothed to Mary and was not looked upon askance because of her being with child. The angel told him not to put her away, as one having extra marital affairs, but to keep on loving her as this matter was divine).

The King remains with the Shulamite for a while but again invites her to accompany Him on His journey among the people. How necessary it is for the people to know their future Queen. He desires to share His vast kingdom with her. The only way to accomplish this is to show her, to have her experience the kingdom through his eyes.

Scene IV:

Scene IV takes place in a garden. The King brings his friends to meet his newly betrothed. The garden scene is unique in that it takes place in a literal garden which is symbolic of her heart. The garden of the heart is characterized by the ancient garden scene found in chapter 4:12 to 5:1. They are walking in the garden and enjoying each other.

Something has changed about these lovers; it is a subtle change. Within them is a maturing of relationship. A possessiveness has entered their manner, a somewhat plural ownership that comes with time. In modern terms, they are "into" each other. Their words are much the same, words of love and endearment, but there is a change. He tells her that He cannot think of life without her. She is His garden. He has planted Himself within her very heart. Her thinking reflects His thinking. Her interests are His interests. Growing in her psyche are the themes of His life. Until now, she has been a closed garden, awaiting the time when she would open just to Him. She acknowledges the change in her life. She is not the same person as before. She responds with such depth that He likens her to a fountain of water that has been shut up but now gushes forth. He is delighted with her.

The Shulamite lifts her voice and addresses the four winds of heaven. She calls forth the hard, cold winter to toughen the garden making it impervious to assault. (Israel experiences cold from the North like North America.) Then she calls the South winds to come and blow upon the garden of her heart so that the sweet blossoms will be wafted to her love. In other words, she wants the garden to grow to His liking. She wants to please just Him. She is happy to have His planting. She is rapturous that the garden has produced the things that He admires. She has purposely divested it of all that is displeasing and now nourishes that which pleases Him. The King thinks her to be so faithful and beautiful that He is not content to muse on her just for Himself. He wants all those who know Him to know Her. His friends now enter the scene at His invitation.

He is eager to show her to them, to reveal His romantic partner. He invites them to drink of the fountain of her being. Such an invitation to experience her personality and charm would not be uncommon even today. They rejoice with Him. He has a treasure envied by all.

Scene V:

This is the Search scene. We find the Shulamite in her bedchamber. A joyous day has exhausted her and left her sleeping. She is awakened by the voice of Her beloved. Dripping with the dew of night upon Him, He requests entrance to her room. She, having taken off her street clothes, bathed, and in her bed, calls that she cannot come to the door. She has bathed her feet, and she doesn't want to get them dirty. She bids Him to open the door Himself, and He tries. His hand enters the door panel, but He is unable to gain entrance. Desirous not to override her will, He steps away and reenters the night. Not hearing Him enter, she quickly leaves her bed and rushes to the door. He has departed quietly.

Frustrated with her selfishness, the Shulamite calls for the King in the darkness, and there is no response. Without thinking, she enters the streets with just her night clothes. Again, she meets the Watchman walking the pavement. This time is vastly different. Instead of being treated like an innocent girl seeking her lover, the watchman scrutinizes her with lust. She is ill-attired. He thinks: "Perhaps the King has grown tired of her; therefore, she might be open to my advances." He grabs for her, seizing her garments to tear them from her. He is joined by other watchmen who have observed the fray. Her cries, her struggles are met with blows. Tears are filling her eyes as she seeks to free herself. Indeed, she wrestles herself free from their grip and hurries to the place where she last heard the King's voice, her bedchamber.

Having lost only her dignity and in a disheveled state, the Shulamite sobs in disbelief because of her treatment. Did the men not know she was spoken for? Did they not realize she was betrothed to the King? Did it not matter to them? Racing through her mind are the consequences of having not answered the Bridegroom's call. If she had let Him in and not been so independent, this would not have happened.

While sobbing on her bed, the daughters of Jerusalem take the scene and inquire about the Shulamite's love for the King. They ask her to tell them the reasons she loves Him at all. They summons her response to detail what she thinks of Him. Calculated to solidify determination within her, and partly to draw her away from the event of the street, they ask.

The girl's answer would melt the coldest of hearts. She describes every intimate detail of the Shepherd-King. She has missed nothing. Her descriptions reveal the depth of her desire for Him. She cannot find superlatives rich enough to do Him justice. Finally, she exclaims: "He is altogether lovely. This is my beloved, and this is my friend, O daughters of Jerusalem (5:15,KJV)." (Being a friend as well as lover is a plunge into true love.) Her love is real, and she acknowledges to them just how real.

Still the daughters of Jerusalem question. They seek to draw from the Shulamite a verbal commitment held before many witnesses, but they are halted by another voice. It is the King's voice! He has listened to her testimony of love! He has listened to her descriptions and relished her words. It is now His turn!

The King who does all things well, certainly did this well. He proffers the most beautiful love sonnet of the ages. His descriptions of the Shulamite are intimate revelations of what He sees in her. No longer before Him is a naivete, but a woman. She is a woman of stature in her own right. He focuses on her and reveals that she has more than physical beauty; she is a "prince's daughter," His music parallels hers. They sing to each other chorus after chorus of accolades. Everyone who observes them approves of them. They are made for each other, tailored to meet the needs of the other, a Divine complementarity.

The Shulamite shouts to the daughters of Jerusalem, "I am my beloved's and his desire is toward me (7:10,KJV)." This declaration is cryptic. She reveals to the world that the King's total being is enwrapped in her. He needs her. He loves her. He desires her. He cannot live without her.

Again, the King invites the Shulamite to come with Him. He calls her to "go forth into the fields and lodge in the villages (7:11KJV)." She quickly accepts. There will be no more lonely nights, no more street scenes. She is going to stay by His side day and night forever. Her place is beside Him. Her life is His life; Her interests, His interests. The world will know she has made a quality commitment to Him.

The King and the Shulamite girl enter the villages, and there she meets the multitudes in need. Now she knows why He wanted her to come with Him. He has compassion on them and heals them. Among the people, He goes about carrying out Luke 4 with His anointing on them both. There she learns from Him how to nurture His people. She shares His task; she honors His way of being and doing. She glories in His station and does all that she knows how to assist Him in the way. Her task is not forced on her; she has volunteered! The Law of Love is greater than any other Law. Just as she has witnessed His ministry, she ministers. She lays hands on the sick and they recover. She calls things into being by faith. She hears the pitiful cry of the hurting and meets the need. She is the extension of His being, even when He is not present. The multitudes love and honor her because she is like Him.

SCENE VI:

Preparation begins for a Wedding. The multitudes are gone. The stage is bare except for the Shepherd-King and the Shulamite girl. Just as they began, so the play closes with them alone. The most beautiful words in the text issue from His mouth, but could have issued from Hers as well. A concert of love surrounds them. He says: "Set me as a seal upon thine heart, as a seal upon thine arm: for love is strong as death: jealousy is cruel as the grave: the coals thereof are coals of fire, which hath a most vehement flame. Many waters cannot quench love, neither can the floods drown it: if a man would give all the substance of his house for love, it would utterly be contemned (8:6-7,KJV)." She truly is His pearl of great price!

Secure in her place with the King and now preparing to be joined with Him formally before His father, the Shulamite's attention turns to others. She is concerned that there are many who will not experience all she has experienced and not have the joy she possesses. Here is the eternal theme. He explains that His kingdom is full of many like her, that she is like Eve and represents all who are "in Him." Provision for all who wish is already made.

The Shulamite is satisfied, for she knows, whether present or absent, the Shepherd-King dwells in the garden of her heart and is always with her. Her final words are the cry of the church, "cause me to hear thy voice." The Song ends similarly to Revelation: "Make haste, my beloved, and be thou like to a roe or to a young hart upon the mountains of spices (8:14,KJV)."

EPILOGUE:

This play, reviewed as a whole entity, presents a different picture than its parts. The unfolding of the Song becomes the life story of every believer. Rich in the tapestry of the times, it is now simple to ascertain its meaning. We wonder why it has taken this long. We find the answer in another of Solomon's writings, Ecclesiastes 3:1 (KJV) "To every thing there is a season, and time to every purpose under the heaven." The season for the Song is now.

CHAPTER THREE

A HOLY KISS

"Let Him kiss Me with kisses of His mouth:...(Song 1:2, KJV)"

LISTEN TO THE LADY TALK

After the identity of the Song in verse one, Solomon has the Shulamite burst upon the stage in an electrifying manner. She hurls to the audience a bold statement rather uncharacteristic for ancient times. This woman does not stand in the same place as others in her historic setting. In fact, the woman of the Song is more equalitarian than her counterparts. She assumes a stance of power and draws on the fact that she has been the recipient of His kisses before![1]

Such words and the passion associated with them immediately draw the viewer into the action. The Shulamite's declaration is rife with meaning. She appears on the stage of life, not in a sanctuary. We are not in church. None of the platitudes, prayers, and response-participation is hinted of in these passages. For this reason, Solomon has the Shulamite set the stage. This work is about two lovers who are intimate, personal, and knowledgeable of each other. She wants the Shepherd-King to kiss her! She wants a mouth kiss! She thinks He is the only kisser in the world. She might even attest that once you have been kissed by Him, no other kiss will ever do. The kiss of the world is cheap in comparison.

This lady wants to be intimate. She wants to be possessed by her lover. She wants Him close to her. She calls forth from her emotional treasure of love. "Let HIM kiss ME," opens the door to complete surrender. She represents the essence of the Bride of Jesus who is completely surrendered in her love for Him. Gone are the appropriate behaviors of a church; welcome are the arms of a lover.

---

[1] "Kisses of His mouth:" The Word poured forth to man by Jesus is like kisses covering all of mankind.

Examine this declaration. What is more intimate than a kiss? A kiss supersedes conversation. It reaches into a level of communication beyond the casual. A kiss is a form of "entering into" the being of another. Exactly aimed at the body of believers in the "last days," it is a declaration which ushers in the next step of our relationship to Jesus. There will be no more of the traditional concepts which promote distance instead of closeness. Gone are the formalism of a professional clergy and a humbled laity! Thank God for a kiss!

Let the Shepherd-King be the initiator. "Let Him kiss Me!" This is intimate love. Intimate love is what the garden of Eden was all about: Intimate walks, intimate talks with a God who loves to hear the most trivial mumblings of His creation. Sin blasted that scene but not this one. Sin was taken care of by Jesus, and His kiss initiates a restoration unspoken of until now. No more distance will be tolerated; it is time for "close up and personal."

Distance characterized the Old Covenant voted into being by a congregation of Israel. "Let Moses go to the mountain," was their decision. Instead of an intimate view of the Holy One, it brought them commandments and a tabernacle. Their voting proved what all such voting has proven, that democracy often votes wrong. Theocracy is better. Theocracy sealed with a kiss is much better! It brings back what God intended for His Son, that He would never be cheated out of intimacy. A kiss makes sure the respondents are close, so close that they are aware of each other's breathing. So close are they that the slightest hesitations are deeply regarded. They are closer than a Temple, closer than a church, closer than any theology could portion. Yes, with a kiss spontaneity is the order of the day. Romance is pervasive. Being in love with Jesus calls us to the same place as the Shulamite, "Let Him kiss Me." The Bride of Jesus can require no less.

The fire of passion burns in a kiss. (If you doubt this fact, give a passionless one to your love and see what is the response.) The Bride whom Jesus plans to carry to the Father will not be a passionless Bride. The fire that burns within Him will burn within Her. She has been the recipient of the baptism of the Holy Ghost and fire. They meet each other on the same footing in this quotient. The Shulamite may be criticized in coming verses, but she bears no criticism for her desire toward Him. What centuries of prophets and myriads of life stories could not do, one kiss did. Jesus suffered the cross and gave Himself to have this moment with His bride; there is nothing like His kiss. When you have been embraced by the Son of God, you have been embraced!

This book is unique, for no rabbinical order could have written it. Only the Holy Spirit would dare pen its pages. Solomon yielded as a man, with much understanding of passion and love, to a gift from the Holy One. A kiss is often the door of entrance to more intimate relations. Two people open doors to the will and intention of the other through a kiss. Kisses weave a web of mutual commitment and entwine the participants into a spiritual cohesion. (So spiritual is this act that believers are told to greet one another with a Holy kiss.) In the case of the Shulamite, she echoes the heart of every bride: "I am open to His advance."

When the body of believers becomes the Bride, they are open to Jesus' advances. Lost is their agenda, gone is the kingdom building, for a kiss is enough. His control is more desirous than the world that surrounds. The Shulamite's heart wants to melt under the kiss of the King's lips. Surrender is not loss; it is gain when the one surrendered to is the Son of God. Being held close in His arms, while looking into His eyes and hearing His soft words, is the supreme moment. We were born for this. We are to experience Jesus, not philosophize about Him!

A kiss between a man and a woman introduces a new level to their relationship. It is commitment. It is sharing. It is the beginning stage of union. It moves into the realm of feeling-tone. Although unspoken, its invitation is clear. It says with new meaning: "I feel good when you are this near me, talking to me, loving me, calling me with endearing words. When you kiss me, my focus is on YOU!"

When lovers mouth kiss, a new element is introduced. This is not a handshake, a friendly peck on the cheek; this is a mouth kiss. The mouth kiss declares a relational change. That is exactly the reason it is introduced at the very offset of the Song. Jesus is to have a Bride: Someone He knows and who knows Him. She, who is the second Eve, wants to be kissed by the Second Adam. No, it was never the intention of Heaven for Him to be alone. His walk on earth without a Bride was abstinence for THIS BRIDE!

Notice that the text says: "Let Him kiss Me, with the KISSES of His mouth (1:2)." That means more than one kiss. The Shulamite asks the King to kiss her with all the kisses He wants because she wants them all. In other words, He has permission (act of her will) to kiss and keep kissing. He is welcome. Love is the precursor of claim. She wants his kisses. She is receptive to them. She is a willing and active participant in them. As the kiss is an expression of love, so also is it an expression of approval, investment, and desire. The Shulamite is not unaccustomed to being near Him; she feels no chagrin in her request for a kiss. She is deeply and actively involved with Him. Passivity can never be an accusation cast on the Shulamite. Passivity is for the Church. Active passion is the hallmark of the Bride.

Have you noticed that once the barrier has been broken with a kiss, nothing less is then expected. A kiss establishes a new set of rules governing behavior. Social distance is broken. When the anointed One kisses His anointed Bride, something new is on the scene. Truly, this is the next step, a step beyond all that the body of believers can imagine. A flood is about to take place. A flood of kisses, embraces, and rapturous joy has invaded the day. (I firmly believe that once the true Bride enters into this relationship, voluntarily and vocally as does the Shulamite, she will not be lonely long.) Intercession will be answered by a Person and His kiss.

A kiss symbolizes so many unspoken elements, it is difficult to define. Relative to the individuals, the moment, and the time, a kiss means many different things. Its importance to the Song cannot be lightly touched. At this moment, at this time, with these participants, the kiss means restoration. To understand the <u>Song of Solomon</u>, one must understand the meaning of the kiss, for this will not be the last one.

Restoration is one of the key elements in the latter days. Nothing spells restoration like a kiss. It was the kiss that Jesus spoke of in His treatment of the Prodigal Son. The kiss of the father completely restored, in one action, all that had been lost by the world. His kiss restored favor with the father. His kiss gave vent to conversation thought impossible. Prepared speeches fell to the earth as useless in the wake of a kiss. The prodigal's words were lost in the words of the father calling for the Ring and the Robe. Authority and power were transferred to the prodigal in a flash. Position in the extended family was immediate. If Chapter 1 verse 2 speaks of nothing more, it speaks of this! The Shulamite's lover did not consider her to be anything but fully restored. The verses which come later in this chapter, where the Shulamite expresses a negative view of herself, are not a factor. As His Bride, she has lost the desire to speak in negative terms; her speech flows with positiveness and power.

The Shulamite calls for a kiss! She wants the approval symbolized by it. Her inmost being calls for the warmth and intimacy such a kiss will bring. It, however, must be the Shepherd-King doing the kissing! He is the author of forgiveness and tender love. He established Love to rule over Law. Those who understood Him in this matter broke bottles of ointment and bathed His feet, toweling them with their hair. Those who did not understand this entreated Him with doctrinal statements and dilemmas of religion. The same is true today! Those who understand Jesus "lean upon His breast." Those who do not understand Him choose, like Judas, to kiss Him rather than be kissed by Him.

Tenderness is in a kiss. Fear is melted away in a kiss. A kiss melts distance and destroys timidity. "Knowing" is the established order, rather than just a "knowing about." Remember, Solomon took a trek into history by moving the Israelites away from a "tent of meeting" to a Temple. The destiny of such a move precluded a time when men would know a great deal more about Law than about Love. The time came when they held more closely to their traditions than the Treasure. When Jesus was birthed in this earth, He came as a judgment to all that established religion had become. He would not restore it to its former day when God tabernacled with men through clouds and fire, but He established a new order based on the Law of Love. This allowed men to enter the heavens and walk with fire.

What more is to be found in this kiss? It shows this is a "kiss" relationship: Very close, very tender, extremely personal, and warranting care. However, this is not the sum of the relationship; it is the platform for the relationship. Built on caring, embodying I Corinthians 13, it challenges all other life relationships. Once understood, this standard becomes the new base for walking with Jesus. No longer will distance reign. No longer will He be simply enthroned in power at the right hand of God the Father. He will be enthroned in our hearts as well. "Let Him Kiss ME," is the cry of our being. Knowing we desire this intimacy even if it be afforded to only one believer on earth, we cry out "let us be the ONE!" If this be selfish, then let it stand!

Kisses will surely fall away to possession, and here lies the crucible. Jesus is possessed of us, and we are possessed of Him. It was this "mutual-possession" that led Him to a cross where love was written in hands of blood. The sacrifice of Calvary is a sacrifice for a loved one. Because He saw by faith a redeemed, pure, and spotless Bride waiting for His kiss, He died. O, the kiss formed by this kind of love has ingredients unimagined by mortal intellect. What is spoken in these passages cannot be ascertained by mind pursuit. All the biblical studies of a million institutions cannot develop in the heart what can be accomplished by a kiss! Universities cannot comprehend the study of such heart-love. Bearing in His body the scars of His trials, Jesus holds triumphantly that which is the Prize. My God, when we read the passage: "Husbands love your wives, as Christ loved the CHURCH," how differently does it read. Church is no longer viewed as a cathedral or convention; it is viewed from the prospect of the Bride.

"Let Him kiss me," is heard above the sound of organs, choirs, and preachments. Its call is the call of those ready to embrace Jesus on His terms, not their own. His agenda is written in us. That is very different from searching for an agenda of our own. Our call will be answered; the Shulamite's was. It is the "virgin-call" of those whose lamps are trimmed. It is the call of those whose oil is richly stored, who long in the night and through the day for His touch, His kiss, and His voice. Just as the Temple was replaced by the cloven tongues of fire, so the present legalism will be vanquished with a kiss!

It was the desire of our Lord to institute a deeper form of communion than a cup: it is His kiss. He told His disciples He would not participate in such a supper until He did so with them in heaven. One communion will call for the other. A marriage is going to take place, and the communion supper will be sealed with a kiss. Cryptic words were these words. Unwilling to commit communion to be institutionalized by doctrine, He determines the time and place for its true consummation. The New covenant is a Bride thing. Romans 5 says it is. When the first bride fell into the pit of sin and grasped the hand of the first Adam, sin entered the world. Behold, the second Adam grasps the hand of the second Eve, and righteousness goes beyond sin to cancel every debt.

Note how the Shepherd-King's kiss melts distance and timidity so His bride be drawn into a new order. Unwilling that she remains untrained, ignorant, and unfulfilled, He begins with a kiss. He is the kisser. He is the initiator. His is not seduction's path; His is tenderness which leads to an awakening with no sorrow. His lessons end in joy. His teaching calls for more teaching. His kiss calls for more. "Let Him kiss Me with the kisses of HIS MOUTH," for He who spoke worlds into existence surely breathes a different sigh in His kiss! His love lessons begin with acceptance. They draw on her to respond and, with each response, carry her into new levels of understanding. Each level requires her permission, for her will is never violated. She is surrounded with His love and through their interaction will be drawn into His nature. Romans 5:17 says it clearly:

> "For if by one man's offence death reigned by one; much more they which receive abundance of grace and of the gift of righteousness shall reign in life by one, Jesus Christ." (KJV)

"...THY LOVE IS BETTER THAN WINE. (SONG 1:2B,KJV)"

Once Jesus paid Hosea's ransom (The thesis of Hosea is that He bought back his bride and restored her to His bosom in much the same way that Jesus paid the price at Calvary to redeem man back to God.), His bride could forthrightly declare the next part of this opening verse: "for thy love is better than wine." The wine in this case is synonymous to living her own life in the "world." The world's love is illicit and filled with selfish intent. It took a Saviour to illustrate the difference God intended for us to experience in love. Once knowledgeable of the difference, our heart cry is: "Enough, I am finished with the illicit love of a world without Him!" Jesus' love does not have the illicit character of this world's lust. The Bride knows the difference and says so in this verse. The Church, without question, considers itself to be the Bride. This is taught in theology classes and generally accepted by the world of denominationalism. However, the delineation between the Bride and the Church begins at this point. The Bride knows the difference between His love and that of "world love." Ezekiel addressed the exact dilemma in his day. Ezekiel 44 shows the difference in clear terms. Ezekiel asked God why He allowed Priests and Levites to continue in office when He (God) knew of their offences and sins. God said the errant priests and Levites could continue ministering to the people but could not come near to Him or minister to Him. Declarations on the Sabbath by a defiled priesthood did not penetrate the heavens, nor will they for the Church. Friendliness with the world becomes enmity with Him. He isn't going to kiss some battered up old rag of a thing. The bride cannot sip the wine (the life) of the world and hope the drops won't stain her robe. She cannot sit in the bar of Satan, in Cafe Hell, and wink at the waiter only to hurry home to Jesus' kiss. There has to come a definite time in her life when the drunken language of the earth, characterized by the salacious innuendoes of its seducers, will be ignored. She has to determine whose house she will live in, whose kisses will satisfy, whose love is the greatest. His love supersedes the fantasy-based media-determined worldly love. His is holy love. Holy love is different in degree and kind than earthbound love. This is love generated from a different base. Its foundation is in heaven; its source is the Son of God. Love has to designate its source, which is an integral part of its nature. The Shulamite indicates its source is in Him. "His love is sweeter than wine," designates the source of this love and declares the difference is in Him. What makes His love different?

The Greeks used nine different words which are ultimately translated as "love." They revealed the source and the type of love being discussed by using different words. Jesus used this technique as a base for questioning

Simon Peter at the end of His ministry. Jesus' "Lovest thou me?" called for Simon to answer in kind, but he did not. If a lover whispers to his beloved, "I love you with all my heart," a response equal to the sincerity and depth of the declaration is expected. If the respondent flippantly replies, "Yeah, I love you too," one does not need a dictionary of words to comprehend.

The expression of love seeks an answer in kind, although it may be comprehensive enough not to be limited by whatever answer it receives. The Shulamite calls for the Shepherd's kisses and declares His love to be sweeter than wine. Her declaration will be responded to in kind and fervor. Jesus is like that! Her human and spiritual need is Him. Jesus is truly the only one who can fulfill that need. Remember this work is based on a human plane, and it meets humanity in the human dimension. Jesus loves His Bride when she is on the earth. The Bride needs a love relationship with Jesus while she is here.

That mankind craves a love relationship at all is proof enough that God created its portent within the human heart. What we hear in the Shulamite's declaration is something a human can express. The Song is not based on some ethereal state. The Song's power is manifested in the now. Its setting is earth not heaven. Its teachings are for our preparation to step higher in THIS life. The Song targets the heart of the reviewer. If the reader is the true Bride, he or she will be strongly drawn into and captured by its power. If the reader has no ears with which to hear or eyes with which to see, then the book means nothing.

One cannot remain a spectator and complete the Song's purpose. When we step onto the stage and cry "kiss me," and exclaim "thy love is sweeter than wine," at that moment victory will swell within us. The painting of Solomon is not some museum piece locked in antiquity's closet. It is a now-work. Many believers have come from the closet of prayer and sweet communion with Jesus shouting, "Your love is sweeter than wine."

Those who reeled out of the upper room already knew more than the world that observed them. Overflowing with the wine (the new life) of His outpouring, filled with the same Spirit which filled Him, they entered the streets. They knew the wine of His love. Whether early disciple or modern saint, all have to come to a conclusion of their own: "Thy love is better than wine (than the life of the world)." No one can make that commitment for another. Every mouth must confess it. When we say it with our mouths, as a witness to ourselves and the world, something changes within us. We crystallize our testimony and reinforce our conviction to have His love is a greater asset than any offer of "world-wine."

Libations of pleasure, worldly scenarios of fleshly satisfaction characterize worldly wine. The wine of the world promises but cannot fulfill its pledges. It offers but cannot carry through. Drink of its Epicurean, humanistic potion, and you will find the drug dregs of death. "Senseless avenues leading to pointless waste" is what the illumined mind of the Bride sees. Jesus' love is sweeter to the taste, to the palate, to the mind than the whole of earth's allure compressed into its wine. Joy unspeakable cannot be found within the world's gates or by imbibing the world's wine.

For the true Bride, there can be no fellowship with the world nor with its social or religious expressions. Most of the world's avenues of expression, its music, its philosophies, its media trivia, slip passed her ears. She has been with One whose voice is all the music she will ever desire. His teachings overreach the best of philosophies. His ways bound past present condition to a place called Faith. Here, He lives. Here, She lives. Both observe the earth from a jaundiced viewpoint, a viewpoint often not shared even with religious groups and powerful denominations. She is the Bride redeemed, and she recognizes there is no such thing as passive agreement with the world.

The Bride is aware of Satan and his desire to delude, to deceive, and to cause death. As he has been, so is he still. Whether camouflaged with piousness or flagrant in its demeanor, Satan's worldliness still smells of him. His most deceptive delusions are found in the most pious places. His Judases abound. His "painted sepulchers full of dead men's bones," still elicit her Lovers' wrath. Jesus' love surpasses anything this world has to offer whether it be found in sanctuaries or seductions; His love is better than wine! From her position of glory, she can think of nothing but HIM. She has been transformed by the renewing of her heart, mind, and soul. She is consumed with her love for Him. How different this is from "the church" assembled in many places on this earth; they are consumed with their own perpetuity.

A worldly church, filled with the unredeemed and manned by the unspeakable, has no concept of the words of the Song. To them it is a pleasantly tuned erotic piece of literature unfit for study, only to browse. To the Bride, it is the essence of her Being exposed in passionate intimacy her "under-oiled" sister will never experience.

How beautiful the Shulamite (Bride) is. Standing framed in glory at the very opening of Solomon's work, she parallels the woman of Revelation Twelve. The woman with the twelve stars gave birth to the Shulamite's lover (Jesus) and is giving birth to the rest of the many-membered body of Christ that will rule the nations with a rod of iron. This woman represents the Jerusalem from above that is "the mother of us all."

Why does Solomon have the Bride standing like one triumphant at the very beginning of His Song, then flash back to a time when she was not? She opens the book in splendor, for she is complete in Him at this point. She is pointing back to the elements, both in interaction and time, which have made her what she is. Her words are carefully chosen to reflect her new position in Him, and through them she reveals her oneness with Him. Summarized in her opening remarks are the ingredients planted in her heart by her lover. In this context, her comment about His love being better than wine is associated with the end of the book rather than her early expressions in Chapter 1:5. She echoes the theme spoken near the end of the book, "his desire is toward me (7:10)." She verbalizes her desire for Him. Who is like unto this woman in all of history? In her power she exudes humility.

"Your love is sweeter than wine," puts the focus on the King, not the Shulamite. The Holy Spirit has taught her well! He has taught her "His love" is the best love. It is His love which can be depended on. Paul penned similar words in Romans 8: 38-39.

> "For I am Persuaded, that neither death, nor life, nor angels, nor principalities, nor powers, nor things present, nor things to come, Nor height nor

depth, nor any other creature, shall be able to separate us from the love of God, which is in Christ Jesus our Lord." (KJV)

In the chapters ahead, the kind of love spoken at the beginning will be examined and revealed. The Shepherd-King's love will draw the Shulamite; never will He drive her to a decision. His love will honor her will. His love will draw a plan and request her to join Him in it. His love will continually reach out to her. His love will epitomize I Corinthians 13 to the letter. His love is unconditional. His love protects her by thinking ahead and making preparation for her. His love offers her the best of His world. Is it any wonder she can only be satisfied by His kisses and unhesitatingly declares His love to be the best?

"...THY NAME IS AN OINTMENT POURED FORTH, ...
(SONG 1:3,KJV)"

The Shulamite (bride) knows connected to the King's love is the power of His Name (Nature). She has experienced His Name in action in the villages where she has traveled with Him. (Again, these opening passages are reflections of experiences which have brought her to maturity.) She wears the fragrance of His Name on her person. She has been with Jesus, and no Petrine denial is hidden in her heart. His perfume fills the atmosphere around her. His Name on her lips produces an ointment to a world of need. Walk into the most putrefied condition in His Name (Nature) and His Presence will change it. Mary of Bethany's act, which Jesus declared would live as a memorial to her forever, is found in this verse. "His Name is like perfume poured out," (Amplified Version 1:3) is directly connected to her act. When she offered the spikenard and its perfume bathed the room, she loosed what scripture declared a thousand years before. She poured her libation on the liberator. His Name introduced into any situation of the devil denounces him and changes the course of the accursed.

So special is Jesus' Name Paul wrote of it in Philippians. After Paul spoke of His selfless death (like an ointment poured forth), he wrote:

'Wherefore God also hath highly exalted him, and given him a name which is above every name: That at the name of Jesus every knee should bow, of things in heaven, and things in earth, and things under the earth." (Philippians 2:9-10 KJV)

The Shulamite learned, while walking with the Shepherd-King on the mountains and working with Him in the valleys, His Name changes things. No sickness, no poverty, no depression can withstand the power of His Name. In Acts 3:1-16, we are told Peter and John took His Name and cured the lame. So charged were their surroundings, multitudes heard the gospel as the healed man clung to them. They hurriedly avowed it was not their magical charm that healed him but the power of Jesus' Name. The Bride comprehends the power of His Name and weds it to His love.

In Revelation 19:13, Jesus' Name is called "The Word of God." The Word speaks to His Bride, and she knows His word is His bond. The marriage covenant between Jesus and His bride gives her the authority to use His Name. She can apply it to any wound and find the healing balm of Gilead. As an ointment with curative qualities, His Name, when applied to the wounded spirit, brings healing. His anointing, spoken of in Luke 4, demands it. He is anointed by God the Father to "heal the broken hearted." That anointing reaches to the poor, the blind, the captive, and the oppressed. The anointing on Him is now on her. She has entered into the Divine Right to use His Name (Nature) in the situations of her life. With boldness she claims His territory to be hers. She is Divine, Divinely chosen, Divinely appointed, Divinely shaped for just this purpose. She stands as the Divine bride of the Divine Lord of Heaven and Earth.

Further proof of the Divine nature of the Bride's words is found in Deuteronomy 10:20:

"...you shall serve Him and cling to Him, and by His name and presence you shall swear."
(Amplified Version)

Deuteronomy joins hands with the Song, and both link to Philippians. So intertwined is the Word of God no conflict is found in its texts. Those who search for the reason the Song remains in the Holy Writ should search no further than verse 3. Here, the earliest verses point to Jesus.

It is in verse 3 the Bride calls to mind how she would savor the Shepherd-King's Name. This is like the young girl so enamored of her boyfriend she repeatedly writes His Name along with hers. Is this not the nature of lovers? Many times a young girl, contemplating how her name will look with "Mrs." in front, will pen her new name endearingly. Carved on trees, written on rocks, sketched in sand are the dual names of hundreds of lovers. There is something greatly romantic about the public use of the other person's name. It proves an ownership beyond acquaintance. "Judy loves Michael," encompassed by a heart drawn with an arrow, is common place. Can we fault the Shulamite for doing the same?

The Bride is identified with Jesus' Name. She, who has been held close to Him, who smells his special fragrance on her clothes, in her hair, on her pillow, now savors the delicacy of His Name. This Song contains all the expressions of falling in love with Jesus. She has savored Him! Solomon, who knew Psalms 34:8, "O taste and see that the Lord is good," also knew the difference between tasting and savoring. To savor is to give oneself over to the enjoyment of a taste or smell. To surrender to its fragrance is the essence of being saved. Paul wrote in II Cor. 2:15-16:

> "For we are unto God a sweet savour of Christ, in them that are saved, and in them that perish: To the one we are the savour of death unto death; and to the other the savour of life unto life."(KJV)

Would to God the church could have such an identity! That the fragrance of Jesus' presence was on every person in every congregation. That His Name should be spoken by each soul in terms of the precious. That loving Him was on every lip and every thought was of Him. That His Name was used in power by every soul in every pew. Then, the church might begin to call itself, "The Bride."

Sadly it was Jesus who pointed out the problem. His parable of the ten virgins marked a dividing line between those who would enter in and those who thought they might enter in. Not until the last moment, when the shout that the Bridegroom comes, will the final cut be made. Five foolish virgins who had no oil were left weeping and wailing in His parable. They were told to hurry and buy oil if it were possible. They discovered it was not possible.

Having the name for being the Bride is not the same as having the Name of the Bridegroom. To possess His Name begins here on earth, and those who hesitate to take it will find the door is shut. His Name is precious to the true Bride. It is hallowed in her heart where the garden of her lover grows under the perfume of His planting (4:12-5:1). Possession is found in His Name; authority is found in His Name; privilege is found in His Name. Psalms 91:14-16 says:

> "Because he hath set his love upon me, therefore will I deliver him: I will set him on high, because he hath known my Name. He shall call upon me, and I will answer him: I will be with him in trouble: I will deliver him, and honour him. With long life will I satisfy him, and shew him my salvation."
>
> (KJV)

Jesus' Name is poured forth: Poured out at Calvary, poured out on the day of Pentecost, and poured out on the last generation. It is to this generation the Song is written. The rallying point of end-time believers is the Name: Jesus. Doctrines fall away, disassociative behavior crumbles, and barriers disintegrate at His Name. Truly, the "virgins love thee." Those virgins with oil in their brightly burning lamps, with garments clean and spotless, with hearts overflowing with love for Him, will surely be taken with Him. Bathed in the good ointment, refreshed with the perfume of His presence, they <u>run</u> to Him showering Him with their love.

"DRAW ME, WE WILL RUN AFTER THEE:..."[2]
(SONG 1:4, KJV)

Indeed, the virgins will run to Jesus in the final hour of history. They deserve to be drawn into His bosom. The Bride is the second Eve, and she is representative of

---

[2] What are the things we have to be drawn from? Is it not mainly self? The darling sin? Astorath?

all those who are like her. Perhaps this explains the intermittent use of "we" and "me" in verse four.

Editorial use of the word "we" often confuses the reader. Do not let this happen. Speaking in play form, the Shulamite acknowledges the daughters of Jerusalem's presence by using "we." She also uses a flash back to reflect on the reason for her exclamation spoken at the beginning.

"The king hath brought me into his chambers" is the reason for all the former statements. Everything that has been said up to now is predicated on this fact. The Shulamite knows what it is to be <u>with</u> the King. The daughters of Jerusalem join her in that agreement. They know it was the King who did the drawing. They know being drawn into His chambers has made a difference in their lives. The King's chamber is an intimate place. Intimacy is the theme of this work. Acknowledging the truth of her statements, they add their "amen." They know the difference between being acquainted WITH the King (knowledgeable of His works) and being IN the King's chambers.

"Draw Me," coincides with "kiss me." It is a declaration of desire. These daughters (who may represent the Wise Virgins) join with the Shulamite in her request to be drawn. Any person so drawn into the chambers of the King will do the same. The true Bride urges all who will hear to: "Call for Him to draw them into the chambers. There, you will never forget the experience nor desire any greater one." When you have been with the best, you leave the rest! Although the pull of the world summons constantly to conform to its self-centered path, the call of the chamber has greater appeal.

"Draw me," as a solitary phrase, indicates something deeper in scope than meets the eye. It is the framework of the relationship between Jesus and His beloved. Institutions demand; Jesus draws! "If I be lifted up, I will DRAW all men unto me" is not some ethereal jargon. The drawing power of our Lord is down-scaled too often as pulpits focus on their spotlighted productions. Just as the Word of God is sent forth to do what it was commanded to do, so Jesus will draw all men when he is lifted up. This is a Biblical Law: Lift up Jesus, and He will draw men to Him.

Drawing is different from demanding. It is important to comprehend, at the very offset of the Song, the base of the relationship is built on drawing and its response. Nowhere will you find demands made to the Bride. At no point, in this epic account of the union of the Lord to His Bride, will there be a coercive taint. When this is understood, then it is easy to ascertain this work is not built on ancient mores or relations, it is designed for the last days. It supersedes the time in which it was written and bounds across centuries to our own time. Equalitarianism was not a right for women in Solomon's day, but Jesus has always been a gentleman.

As "draw me" compared to "direct me" is a primary ingredient spoken early in the treatise, it is necessary to examine its function. First, it lays a ground rule for the drama. The observer will have multiple opportunities to see the Shepherd-King offer the Shulamite many invitations to join Him. Not once does He demand her to follow. Second, the words "draw me" coming from the mouth of the Shulamite establish a mode of response to a call of need. Having been drawn into His presence before, she again wishes Him to take the lead and "draw me." The vast majority of the encounters Jesus had in the New Testament were based on such a call from another. The call of the disciples, the Samaritan woman, and Zaccheus were the major exceptions. When Jesus hears the "call," answers are coming! Third, "draw me" shows a willingness to be drawn. How important such an attitude is to Jesus. When she makes her request, she mentions no parameters. No question is asked about place, time, nature, or dimension of the domain into which she will be drawn. Time is defenseless in such an appeal. How different is "draw me" to "I command you." The former is humble and submissive; the latter is based on power, status, and moment.

When the Song unfolds and you view it from its conclusion, then it will be easy to see why the Shulamite (Bride) wanted to establish the basis of "draw me." She, who had been drawn from the banquet room of ease and provision to the rugged outposts of service, knows what "draw me" included. She, who through selfish ignorance had encountered the darkness of this world, knows the consequences of not following the "drawing." She has experienced a graphic portrayal of what it means to respond to the Holy Spirit. The Holy Spirit often chooses to utilize the method of "drawing" instead of commanding. This is a major difference between "servants" and "friends". The heart cry of every believer, having been drawn into the chamber of Jesus' presence, is "draw me."

"...THE KING HATH BROUGHT ME INTO HIS CHAMBERS:..." (SONG 1:4,KJV)

This is the gospel invitation! It is the gospel witness! The call into Jesus' chamber means union with Him. Doesn't I Corinthians address this union? After explaining the type and depth of Jesus' love, Paul addresses the effect of that love. He teaches once having experienced union with Jesus, nothing in your life is the same. Paul says seeing "in part" will fall away when we see Him face to face. Being face to face is "up front and personal." Being in His presence is better than hearing about Him. Being in His presence is better than reading about Him. Being in His presence changes US! Those who come into His presence join an exclusivity unknown to others. They join ranks with those who also have been there and are included in the "we" of the Song.

It is the "we" group who are glad and rejoice in Jesus. Unhesitatingly, the "we" group is happy for all who are drawn into His presence. Joy fills the "we" group when they hear of another person so drawn. We who are in that group relish the initiation of another into the joy of His presence. We are gleeful to hear one more soul explode with love for Him and say, "We will remember thy love more than wine." The wine of the earth dims the memory; the wine of His presence refreshes the mind. We rejoice, not because of the great honor or the wonderful invitation to enter His chambers, but we rejoice in Him. It is Him and Him alone who is the theme of our Song; it is He who is worthy of praise.

The praise of those who have experienced Jesus' chamber is vastly different from the songs of those who have not! Give me a choir of the "we" group or a congregation of the "we" group anytime! They sing a different song, offer a different praise, and conduct themselves in a different manner. His chamber changes us, for His presence rejoices us.

Those who invite the church to "practice His presence" have reached for the touchstone of the Song. Here lies the beginning of the creation of one's own private Song. No song ever heard before will be like this song. (I once listened to a group of singers who sang that the song of the angels is beautiful, but "the greatest song of all is the song of the Redeemed." This Chamber music is not the same as earth's chamber music. Its range is wider. It includes the soft whispers of love and the fullness of His joy.

"We will remember thy love," verse 4 says and remember it with joy! What do we remember? We remember the intimate talks known only to us, those talks which take place in the chamber of Jesus' presence. All things are open in the chamber—for nothing needs to be hidden. His heart and our hearts are open to one another.

No agenda is to be found in the spontaneity of Jesus' chamber. Relaxed in His presence, we are open to Him and He is open to us. The secrets of His heart are revealed in His chamber. The plans of His kingdom are made clear in the chamber. The future of our lives is revealed in His chamber. The clouds of doubt and fear never enter His chamber. Peace is always in His chamber.

The Holy Spirit draws the believer into Jesus' chamber, and there He makes clear those things of the future and brings to remembrance every word spoken by Jesus. The Song of Solomon is a continual drawing into greater fellowship with the King. It is a continuum which begins with this very invitation to be drawn into His chamber and goes all the way to Chapter Eight, where the Bride is made ready for the marriage. This invitation to the chamber prepares the reader for the action of Chapter Two, where we view the activities of the Banquet Hall.

In Chapter Two, the audience will see the inner chamber. I call it the "banquet-hall" experience. Foreshadowing the banquet hall scene in her own life, the Bride prepares the audience through verse 4. The banquet hall scene signals the beginning of the Shulamite's spiritual understanding. Here, she is initiated to the vastness of the King's provision. This is the starting point for her personal revelation. (Every believer must enter such a place with Him.) Considering this experience, coupled with all the others of the Song, the Shulamite forthrightly shouts, "The upright love thee!" She is now ready to tell the world how she fell in love with Jesus, for verse 5 begins the phase of "recalling the past."

CHAPTER FOUR

HOW IT ALL BEGAN

"Tell me, O thou whom my soul loveth,...(Song 1:7, KJV)"

"I AM BLACK (dark), BUT COMELY,... (SONG 1:5,KJV)"

How different verse 5 is from the previous verse. Ending the opening scene, we view the completed Bride speaking words which usher into life all the other acts of the Song. Beginning with this verse, we see the Shulamite "shepherd girl" of the past.

Standing on the stage is the shepherd girl, not the completed Bride. The scene is pastoral, and we view young goats (kids) all around her. The blazing sun beats down on her young body. Alone in her work, she has plenty of time to think and muse about her plight in life. Her self-contemplation leads her to despair over her condition and station in life. The audience is privileged to her inner thoughts. The audience hears her inner person being verbalized and thereby gains insight into her secret self.

The girl faithfully tends the goats and thereby fulfills the role to which she has been assigned. Clearly, she is not pleased with the assignment and its consequences. Judging from her anger toward her older brothers, we ascertain they are the ones who assigned her to this work. In this setting, her self-appraisal is based on conditions which surround her. She has poor self-esteem and feels neglected and unappreciated.[1] She opens the scene with: "I am black, but comely...as the (black goat skin) tents of Kedar, as the curtains of Solomon." In other words, she

---

[1] As the Shulamite was saved from a poor self-concept, we are all saved from self-circumstances that would cause our ruin. Jesus ends the bondage to the tasks of our "brothers." The world has many tasks and burdens prescribed for us that we are simply saved from by going with Jesus. True freedom can only come when we are delivered from these "tasks." So much of the world's church work is nothing for than tending "goats" so our brothers can do other things. So many of religions' "duties" have nothing to do with Jesus and His plan. Yet we must remain faithful to whatever responsability we have been given until Jesus calls us to "come away with Him."

knows she is healthy and has good form, but the conditions around her have reduced her appeal to others.

Sun-baked, wind-blown, and tending goats is not the shepherd girl's perception of an ideal setting. Instead of enjoying social events with other youth, she is hidden away by her work. Resentment has built up deep within her spirit. This is how her story begins: A lonely girl full of resentment, thinking self-deprecating thoughts while attending goats.

The Shepherd Boy later on will deal with these aspects marvelously. His handling of them depicts Jesus and His attitude toward believers. Clearly, He disregards much of the girl's verbal disparagement and focuses on what He sees in Her. He forces her to look at herself through His eyes. Slowly she will arrive at a different self-image. Soon, she will modify all of her self-concepts to reflect his positive reasoning and will not be ruled by what she sees. Pictured for us in this scene is a microcosm of all the world and its militating circumstances. The world all of us live in is cruel, and its circumstances lead the us to wrong conclusions about God and ourselves.

From center stage the Shulamite admonishes the audience not to look on her. "Look not upon me, because I am black, because the sun hath looked upon me (Song 1:6 KJV)" is her appeal. Wrapped in this appeal is an errant self-appraisal. She wishes she were presentable enough to be looked on in favor. She desires that suitors would be pleased with her visage rather than appalled by their view. "If only" is the term which predicates her life. "If only," I could have time to coiffure my hair, anoint my skin, care for my person, then things might be different, she reasons. "If only, I was not given this responsability for others that forces me to choose between caring for myself and caring for others." She seeks to place the blame on others for her plight. She places the blame on her "brothers" who were angry with her. She places blame on them because "they made me the keeper of the vineyards."

Why does the shepherd girl choose the word "vineyard" rather than goats? Later in the Song there will be other references to vineyards. It will be clear at this point why she chose this metaphor. It does, however, emphasize the creative technique used by Solomon to introduce themes as precursors to future events. Every word of the Song fits the reference in Proverbs to a "word fitly chosen." For now, her reference to the "vineyard" is used to compare her work with her person. She is busy taking care of others and is not taking care of herself. In the future text, her vineyard will be the King!

Solomon allows us to see the condition of the "Bride-to-be" <u>before</u> intimately knowing the Shepherd-King. It is not a pretty sight! However, she will not long remain in this state of mind or work. Like Joseph, she is about to leave the prison and take on even greater responsibility.

The Church reels under the cares of life and the lies of the devil. In the lonely hours, Satan delights to point out our sad state of affairs. He gloats when, out of our own mouths, we speak words like the Shulamite. He gleefully shouts when, in a state of depression, we almost despair of life. He points to a myriad of remedies to relieve the pain, but he never points to the One who is the Healer. That is not his plan. Keeping the Church focused on itself, wallowing in self-pity, and dreading the night is his delight.

The Shulamite speaks for all humankind in her soliloquy of the soul! Damned by circumstances, the world looks for a place to hang the blame. Blasted by the elements, disheveled by the winds of (what they call) Fate, the majority of the world awaken to carry out their tasks daily with a sense of despair. Their cry is the cry of the shepherd girl, "Don't look at me," and they add to that, "don't touch me." Being left alone may be the outward will, but the inner man weeps because there is no one to touch or care.

Darkness shrouds the stage, although it is midday in the scene. (Contrasts and comparisons fill the Song.) Darkness at midday is what happened on the cross. Darkness and Light are always in battle, for such are the themes of the world's greatest literature. It is the struggle of our souls to wrestle with the darkness and cry for the Light. Solomon weaves such "soul-struggle" into the fabric of his work beginning with this scene. Pathos enters through the Shulamite's voice which is raised to the audience in the style of grand opera. Directed to the audience, her soul is bared. (The Song often bares her soul in sequence after sequence.) If the church is to be the Bride, let her then be honest! The end times hold no place for charades. Someone needs to intercede for the world's ecclesiastical state of affairs; he needs to intercede somewhere between the porch and the altar. He needs to intercede with tears. Someone needs to bare the soul, not to a world sick of hearing the church's misdirection, but to the only One who can do something about it. "Somebody Help Me," is the cry which can only be answered by the "I AM who can!"

"TELL ME, O THOU WHOM MY SOUL LOVETH, WHERE...
FOR WHY SHOULD I ..." (SONG 1:7B,KJV)

How glad I am that Solomon introduces the Shepherd Boy (King Jesus) in this way and at this time. Just when the Shulamite is in her dark reveries, she spies a man on the horizon. He is beautiful to look on. He is handsome in His manner and His walk. He knows where He is headed![2]

Yes, I am aware the feminists say a man is not the answer, but sometimes he is, especially if he is the man whom God has sent to be your lover forever. This is a good place to review a few facts. First, the Shulamite is honoring her mother and the need of her family by tending her goats. She is obedient like a servant. Second, by being faithful over little, she is about to be faithful over much. Third, it is the power of the Mighty God which directs her path into the path of One who will be a source of joy in her life for eternity.

This is not a happenstance meeting. The merging of paths in this scene indicates the merging of lives on a greater scale. True, the pair are portrayed as lowly shepherds, but pent-up inside them is greatness. They have been designed for each other before the foundations of the world. Recognizing the romantic impact of their greeting and meeting is one matter, but recognizing the hand of God in relationships is another. What God did for the Shulamite, He can do for any person seeking a life mate.

---

[1]Notice, people fall in love with Jesus for different reasons. When you reach that point, does it matter the reason? Love is met with love.

Digression is necessary at this point in the commentary. Virtually hundreds of attempts have been made to interpret the Song of Solomon as a marriage guide. Vignettes have been plucked from its pages and projected on the big screen of pulpits drawing almost every conclusion imaginable. I encourage anyone entering these pages to be careful how he or she handles God's Word and revelation. Don't remove statements from context! The Holy Spirit will guide you into great areas of truth through these texts, but let Him be the guide. It is true the passages are beautiful and can be utilized in numerous ways. They can even be used to enhance the romance of any couple. Keep in mind; however, the Song is a book designed to show the Bride and her relationship with Jesus. With that, let us return to the text.

The Shulamite is very aggressive in what is construed to be the opening statement between two strangers: "Tell me, O thou whom my soul loveth, where thou feedest, where thou makest thy flock to rest at noon:...(Song 1:7 KJV)." This statement is rich in its impact. Unlike Ruth who quietly gleaned along the fence row, the Shulamite boldly inquires. This opening line may have two meanings: love at first sight, or familiarity bred by previous encounters. Either view makes no difference. What is important is that her loneliness is gone, and hope rises in her heart. No longer is the issue of unattractiveness a concern, for she has a "significant other" who evidently shares her universe. Who is this Shepherd Boy standing before her?

The Shepherd Boy is not defined or characterized apart from the Shulamite's words. Interestingly enough, conclusions about Him have already been drawn. We know that He is the object of her affection. She uses the words "thou whom my soul loveth" as a declaration.[3] Knowing about her love for him as pictured in the opening lines and established in this meeting, we accept Him because of Her. I draw this to your attention, for this is how the world accepts Jesus now! Born out of the testimony of the believer is the witness the world hears and believes.

---

[3]Revealed revelation begins with a simple inquiry which ends with a romance. I have known scholars who just took a peek into a certain matter and fell in love with it. The Shulamite asked a simple question and wound up falling in love with the Shepherd Boy.

When the Shepherd Boy finally does speak, He is kind and powerful. Clearly, the Shulamite wants to water her little goats alongside His sheep. Romantically, she wants to be close to Him. Psychologically, she might also need the protection of His company. Conjecture need not enter the scene, for what is clear is that she and the Shepherd Boy will be shown together from this point onward.

The poetry of the hour is captured in the repose of the scene. In this setting we see similarity to other settings. Psalms 23 has glimpses of clear water, good pasture, and the Lord being the Shepherd. Similarly, these elements are evident in the scene at hand. The Shulamite chooses a midday rest rather than evening rest because this is the period which best suits her and the Shepherd boy. She is not at the end of her task; she is in the midst of it. Rest at noon is resort's reward. She is portrayed as willing to change her feeding place to that of the Shepherd Boy. She wants to water her flock at the safe water place of His choice. She wants to enter the rest of His rest. Does this sound a little familiar? What would be the desire of the Bride of Jesus if it was not for these things?

"...WHY SHOULD I BE AS ONE THAT TURNETH ASIDE..."
(SONG 1:7B, KJV)

The Shulamite's wording is careful when she adds: "for why should I be as one that turneth aside by the flocks of thy companions?" Why should I turn aside after second hand revelation? Why should I follow after the flocks of your companions when I can be with you? I want to be your companion, not just follow the "flocks of thy companions."

The Shepherd Boy calls her the "fairest among women," then bids her join Him if she pleases. "Go thy way forth," invests decision making power in her. Solomon, however, uses these words to foreshadow the last chapter in the book. What the Shulamite learns from walking with His companions is reflected in Chapter 8. She learns to desire His voice, evenas they do.

When the Shepherd Boy addresses the Shulamite as the "fairest," is He speaking from love's blindness or faith's projection? (Gideon was declared a "mighty man of valour" long before he recognized the fact.) From either postulate you choose, please know He answers her in kind. She declares Him as the love of her soul, and he declares her the most beautiful of women.

Both the Shulamite and the Shepherd Boy will begin to flow into the superlative within the next verses. Showering each other with love words so cryptic that they deserve individual attention, she is being ushered into the banquet chamber of Chapter 2. For now, He invites her to join Him. It is the equivalent of saying: "If you don't know the territory, just pull alongside and we will walk it together!"

"I HAVE COMPARED THEE,..." (SONG 1:9, KJV)

Beware as you enter this section of the Song! Others have entered here and lost themselves and the meaning of its verses. Cleanse your heart; ask the Lord to illumine your mind. Prepare yourself through prayer, and bring your mind into the presence of the Holy Spirit. Often these passages have been trivialized as so much diatribe. Sometimes, even scholars run past these phrases as if they are meaningless. They were not meaningless to Jesus. They were not meaningless to Solomon who carefully placed them as stones are placed in a garden. They are delicately arranged to enhance beauty and offer contrast.

Here Solomon begins a surreptitious weaving of meaning into every word- picture. Although they are arranged as mutual compliments often heard between lovers, they are laden with symbolism. First, take the conversation as it appears in the text. Read through the text down to the banquet scene in Chapter 2:3. The lovers are in dialogue. Although their words emphasize the physical attributes of each other, attention must be paid to each area focused on. Beauty may be in the eye of the beholder, but what is significant to the beholder is of utmost importance. Notice the daughters of Jerusalem interject their comments in 1:11. All other verses are the words of the Shepherd Boy and the Shulamite. Confusion reigns here with scholars who disagree as to who is talking in this scene at any given time. (Observe verse 12 in the KJV, NIV, and Amplified Bible. One group has the Shulamite speaking, while the other translations have the Shepherd Boy.)

Several times mutual sessions of praise to one another appear in the Song. Each time the sessions appear as a grouping, they either follow a turning point in their relationship or foretell such an event. Positioned to give affect to the action of the play, they also add ingredients which could not be ascertained without them. Smells, sights, and sounds are interjected by both respondents. Their comparisons are rife with allusion to other scriptures and have meanings which carry over into the New Testament, although written a thousand years before.

Surface value alone gives these phrases dignity. The speeches are fairly evenly divided. The Shulamite gives six, and the Shepherd Boy speaks five. He dignifies her, lifts her to a higher station than she herself would own. She triumphs in His closeness and His attention to her. Their mutual complementarity is admirable in the human sense, for it is an important ingredient in relationships. They flourish in the detailed attention given to each other. However, this is not the sole reason for their speeches. The words of man are never just words. Notice that at the judgment of man, he must give an account of every idle word. Our mouths are powerful tools for good or evil. Cautioned by James that our tongues are like rudders, bridles, and flame, let us view their words.

It is the Shepherd Boy (King) who begins with: "I have compared thee..." Comparatives are interesting because they allow the individual to choose the references. If a wrong comparison is made, the other party may be offended. If someone compared you to a heap of dirt, that might not be as exhilarating as being compared to a beautiful person or an object of honor.

Solomon makes a masculine choice with feminine qualities. He compares the Shulamite to horses. I will not enter the psychological domain of the relationship between women and horses, but there are recent studies with revealing summations. His decision is really not a poor choice, for the Pharaoh had only the best, the most beautiful, the most well cared for steeds. It is interesting that the Pharaoh is chosen, because the Hebrews owned objects and possessions from their Egyptian exodus. Pharaoh's horses would be powerful, ready for battle, and well disciplined. Would these words be complimentary to a body of believers?

Add to the Shepherd Boy's "horse comparison" the endearing phrase "O my love," and two issues come forth. He endows the Shulamite with qualities not yet fully formed in her. Self-fulfilling prophecy is a term used in psychology which applies here. It means when your expectation of a person is verbalized before his or her possession of that expectation – that person may rise to it, or fall because of it. If you tell a person he or she is a "good-for-nothing-dummy," you have set in motion a scenario which he or she might accept. This person may choose to become what you have said. Our words are important! In like manner, if we point to a worthy attribute within a person in crisis, giving him praise of that attribute, he may accept the direction and rise to the occasion. Solomon chose to set a positive note into action. That note is surrounded by the phrase "O my love." When love encompasses our remarks, they are taken in context.

The second item to examine is Shepherd's love phrase which is a response to the Shulamite's love phrase. She calls to Him with, "O thou whom my soul loveth." He responds with equal passion. The relationship has greatly deepened. Her "O thou whom my soul loveth," is met by His, "O my love."

Wait! Look at what is transpiring! Commitment begins with the Shulamite's public acknowledgment she loves the Shepherd Boy. He meets that commitment with a verbal, public acknowledgment of His love. He is setting the stage for a mutual coming together on a different level than has been present previously. Chapter 2 is in the wings, and it will build a base on these passages. As noted before, these dialogues appear when change is in the offing.

"THY CHEEKS ARE COMELY..." (SONG 1:10, KJV)

The Shepherd Boy continues by complimenting the Shulamite's smile: "Your cheeks (your smile) are beautiful; they show the beauty of your teeth." A beautiful, straight white set of teeth enhances any smile. Don't walk away from this as trivial. When an ancient army was defeated, the victors would break the defeated's teeth. She is not defeated; her teeth are not broken. (Ps. 58:6, which was probably taught to Solomon, speaks of breaking the teeth of the unrighteous.) The Bride is not unrighteous. The

Bride is full of righteousness; she is not defeated; her beauty is a joy for all to behold.

"WE WILL MAKE THEE BORDERS OF GOLD..."
(SONG 1:11, KJV)

The daughters of Jerusalem cannot hold their silence. Observing, like a chorus in an ancient play, they enter the scene. They are used in various capacities in the Song but mostly to show movement between these two lovers. The Shulamite called them to witness early in the Song, and now they cannot be silent. They want to encourage the lovers and enhance the word-picture portrayed by the King.

Willingly, they volunteer to make borders of gold for the Shulamite's skirt and adorn her garments with silver ornaments. They want her to look beautiful. They desire her to lack nothing. Such is the desire of all believers for the saints. Willingly, they sacrifice their time, energy, and resources to enhance the bride. Precious gold and silver are not too good for the Bride. If she is to be arrayed in splendor, then they wish to have a part. Handcrafted, artisan enriched, and specially produced are the items she will wear. Are not these the items which will adorn the Bride of Jesus?

Who knows the identity of the daughters of Jerusalem? Their faces are myriad, and their names are not given. All we know is they are willing participants. Their desire to "enter in" and be a part of what is going on in the work of the Lord is obvious. It is their demeanor we all should adopt! Encouraging the Bride, beautifying her wedding garment, and speaking out for her is identity enough!

"WHILE THE KING SITTETH AT HIS TABLE,..."
(SONG 1:12, KJV)

Verse 12 introduces exotic smell to the scene. "While the king sitteth at his table, my spikenard sendeth forth the smell thereof," are the Shulamite's symbolic words. Her adoration is wafted to the Shepherd-King. On the wings of this ointment her honor and love surround Him. Have you seen lovers so in love they look into each other's eyes and are oblivious to all else? Have you been in an intensely passionate situation where electricity from two lovers charged the atmosphere? This is what is happening here. She charges His atmosphere with her presence. Her love has a uniqueness which catches His attention. Notice that she uses the word "sendeth." Being "sent forth" is a scriptural flag. The disciples were "sent out." The Bible says the word of God is "sent forth" to heal. A specific reason, task, or design is associated with the action of this verb. It is one thing to have an exotic perfume present, but to send it forth as if to accomplish a specific purpose is something else.

One thousand years before the event, Solomon heralds the scene of Mark 14:3:

> "And being in Bethany in the house of Simon the leper, as he sat at meat, there came a woman having an alabaster box of ointment of spikenard very precious; and she brake the box, and poured it on his head."
> (KJV)

Ointment in the Song is sent forth to herald another event which had not yet taken place, an event of history which even His disciples could not fathom. Jesus silences the disciples babble and focuses on the moment and the woman. Could this be the Shulamite reenactment? No, this event is prophetic as was so much of the ministry of Jesus. It fulfills prophecy. Listen to Jesus in Mark 14:7-9:

> "...but me ye have not always. She hath done what she could: she is come aforehand to anoint my body to the burying. Verily I say unto you, wheresoever this gospel shall be preached throughout the whole world, this also that she hath done shall be spoken of for a memorial of her."
> (KJV)

Song of Solomon and this New Testament anointing comprise most of the references to spikenard in the Word. Close examination will discover that spikenard mixture is the perfume of the tabernacle used in the worship services and given to Moses in Exodus 30. Why would this be important? They are linked both in time and history. The reason Solomon places the spikenard in the opening of the Song is to point to the real King. Let there be absolutely no doubt in the mind of reader this Book is about Jesus!

Solomon knows the power of two witnesses. He adds to the witness of the spikenard another ingredient: myrrh. In Chapters 1,3,4, and 5, he repeats the theme. He is unwilling for the reader to forget the centerpiece of his work is the King of Kings. Why myrrh? Again in Exodus 30:23ff, Moses is given the formula for making the anointing oil. He is directed to take care in its measurement. He is further instructed what to anoint with the oil, how it is to be used in the worship of the tabernacle, and the consequence of its misuse.

Myrrh, the primary spice, was mixed with proportionate blends of other spices and oil to form an anointing oil not only for the tabernacle but also for the High Priests. Oil for anointing was sacred. It must not be applied to strangers outside the covenant. It must be applied to the inner treasures of the tabernacle to make them so holy that whatsoever touched them was made holy. The oil of myrrh was on them. It is most necessary for the reader to comprehend the significance of these acts. (The knowledge about the anointing oil will play a part in the understanding of Chapter 5:5.)

The anointing oil was poured on Aaron's head; it ran down his beard and then on the skirts of his garments. He was covered with this spice oil. He operated as one anointed because of the anointing oil. In the office of High Priest, he made sacrifice under the oil of the anointing. He touched the oil; the oil touched him. He touched the implements of the tabernacle. They were sanctified (made holy) by the oil. Jesus operates in the heavenlies as our High Priest under the anointing. Jesus, in Hebrews, is shown to be the High Priest. His ministry is in heaven, having brought His own blood to be placed on the altar. That blood is still THERE.

Solomon uses both ingredients in his descriptions: spikenard and myrrh. One was the perfume of the innermost sanctuary; the other is identified only with the most HOLY of artifacts and offices. Solomon weaves his Song as a tribute to Jesus, identifying Him through the spikenard as King and further identifying Him as the greatest of High Priests. It would behoove the reader to learn what prompted Solomon to take this action.

In the Exodus account, Bezaleel was chosen to bring together the artifacts and the myrrh and spikenard oils. Uniquely, he was not of the Levites but of the tribe of Judah. Jesus was also of the tribe of Praise (Judah). Myrrh was brought to Him symbolically by the wise men, along with gold and frankincense, at His birth. At His burial, Nicodemus brought myrrh to anoint His body (John 19:39).

The first mention of myrrh[4] in the Bible is in Genesis 37 and 43. The merchants who took the betrayed Joseph into their custody and sold him as a slave bore myrrh in their laden stock. When Judah sought Israel to let Benjamin and him go to Egypt to find Joseph, he was told to take myrrh with him. The root of the word myrrh in Genesis has a motherly meaning, and carried that meaning as it was sent for a token to a Saviour of His people. Jesus was sold to strangers by His own disciple and, through His ordeal with those strangers, was anointed with myrrh (oil of the anointing that makes Holy).

Need I remind you Esther was anointed with myrrh for six months as portrayed in Esther 2:12. Remember, myrrh used in the anointing oil made whatever it touched Holy. Esther too, was a saviour of her people. Other places in the word of God show the significance of myrrh in its relationship to Jesus. In Psalms 45, many of the allusions found in the Song of Solomon are present in the text.

> "Thou lovest righteousness and hatest wickedness: therefore God, thy God, hath anointed thee with the <u>oil of gladness</u> above thy fellows. All thy garments smell of <u>myrrh</u>, and aloes, and cassia, out of the ivory palaces, whereby they have made thee glad. <u>Kings' daughters</u> were among thy honourable women: upon thy right hand did stand the <u>queen in gold</u> of Ophir. Hearken, O daughter, and consider, and incline thine ear: *forget also thine own people,* and thy father's house; So shall the *king greatly desire thy beauty:* for he is thy Lord; and *worship thou him."* (Psalm 45:7-11 KJV)

You will notice the many references which practically duplicate the Song passages. The Shulamite is told to forget

---

[4] Myrrh is a very bitter spice and is symbolic of the adversity of the way of the cross.

her past and the family who disdained her. We are told to forget our past and its mistakes, to leave the hurts and ill feelings of anger, and to press into Christ. In the Psalms' passage, she is described as a "queen in gold" which is spoken of in Song 1:11. The gold of Ophir was the gold used in the temple building. The daughters of Jerusalem are described as the king's daughters.

Who but Jesus deserved to have the anointing oil on His garments? Who but Jesus came from the Ivory Palaces? Who but Jesus bore the perfume with aloes and spices mixed with spikenard? Who but Jesus greatly desired the Shulamites' (Bride) beauty?

Let us spend a moment on the word "desire" in Psalm.45:11. This word is also used in Song 7:10. What makes this such a strong word is that this is the first time we are told that Jesus desires His Bride. In the coverage of Chapter 7, I shall show the significance of this phrase. For now, let our attention turn to other passages in the Psalms 45 section.

In the last moments before He died on the cross, Jesus was brought wine mixed with myrrh. Contrast this myrrh with the myrrh brought at His birth. That which was brought at His birth meant "beginning, like the opening of a shaft into a darkness." The flavor of the word myrrh at His death meant "spreading like a sail is spread to the wind." He spread open the heavens; He spread open the way for the Gentiles to be saved, and He spread open Hell's domain and blasted it. The flavor of the word in Exodus, Esther, Psalms, and the Song is the same: "bitterness." The flavor of the word in Genesis was "mother." Now, let us sum up the total picture in four sentences. Like a mother, the Hebrew nation gave birth to Jesus. In bitterness, He bore the sins of the people. In power, He unfurled the flag of heaven in the heavenlies on the earth and in Hell. He is Lord!

"A BUNDLE OF MYRRH IS MY WELL BELOVED UNTO ME;..." (SONG 1:13, KJV)

Keep focused! The symbolism in these opening passages set the pace for other symbolism throughout the text. The Shulamite's comparison of the Shepherd-King to a bundle of myrrh she shall hold between her breasts begs the same exposition as His comparisons of her. She sees Him as total holiness! Keep this in mind. He is! In the Genesis passages, everything that touched the Holy instruments with the holy anointing oil was itself holy. Bundled into one package, this Jesus is all the holiness of God. That little bundle (Jesus) which Simeon held was the embodiment of holiness. Every righteous person who has ever known Jesus wants to hold Him close. Why is the Shulamite different? She is the rightful bride and has a claim on Him.

"...HE SHALL LIE ALL NIGHT BETWIXT MY BREASTS."
(SONG 1:13,KJV)

Get this: **Shall** is not present fact; it is futuristic. It is a prophecy about a future event, but it is as real as if it had happened already by faith. Whatever touches the anointing is holy. The Shulamite wants to touch the anointing and be touched by the anointed One. (The anointing is a discussion so vast it would dilute the power of these verses to study it here. I suggest the reader makes an exact study of the anointing because it will assist him in understanding Biblical texts.) Remember this one fact; there is an anointing that breaks yokes (see Isaiah 10:27). When the Shulamite wills the anointing to be on her like a lover in the night, she wills a yoke breaking power into her life. She wills intimacy which makes entrance to deeper even more meaningful times with the Shepherd-King. The intent of these verses is to show a mental, emotional, and even physical transformation away from a shepherdess toward being a Queen. She wills the metamorphosis spoken of in the New Testament. Metamorphosis is the term used by Paul for every believer changed into a new creature by Christ Jesus (Christ meaning the anointed one with the anointing on Him).

Interaction is a key factor at this juncture. Lying all night between someone's breasts lends itself to something more than formal gibberish. It's what I call "Pillow Talk." "Pillow Talk" with Jesus may not fit your theological dictum, but it did for the Shulamite. She declares the dawning of a new day in thinking about Jesus and the relationship of the Bride to Him. Lying next to the personification of Holiness allows for an intimacy previously unheard of or at least unthought. In such a setting there exists the secret whispers of love like those only known in closeted prayer.

    The bedchamber of the Bride brings the element of mutual possession onto the stage. She possesses the King, His attention, His words of passion, and His love. The church has prayed long, spoken adroitly, sung loudly, but what is missing is the pillow whisper of a lover! To be held in His arms and told what you mean to Him is better than any words of man. (His love words received under these conditions change many things. Worship services, fellowship meetings, and special events hold no sway when compared to intimacy with Him.)

    Communication is face to face in the bedchamber. Communion at this level is the sort spoken of in the Epistles of John. It needs delving into. The word communion, in I John, is better translated by using a Spanish word *compañerismo*. Jesus and the Bride (as described in I John) make the communion services in most churches pale when compared to their *compañerismo*. (Isles of exile proffer a different relationship with Jesus than 10 minutes of prayer and Bible study just before dashing to the workplace.)

    Lie all night with the holiness of Jesus' Word drawn closely to your breast and see if the dawn doesn't look better! Whisper throughout the darkness your innermost thoughts and desires, and discover the swiftness of the morning. Put your arms around Him and tell Him how much you love Him. It will make a bride out of a grown man! Metamorphosis![5]

"...CAMPHIRE IN THE VINEYARDS OF ENGEDI."
(SONG 1:14, KJV)

    The Shulamite continues her comparisons. She says that the Shepherd-King is like "a cluster of camphire in the vineyard of Engedi"(Song 1:14). Camphire is a

---

[5] Think about how hard it is for a man to percieve himself as the bride. At first I found it difficult to imagine a 6'4" fellow like myself ever coming to a place other than a "brother," never a "bride." The transformation into a bride is a psychological thing. Whole attitudes have to change. Whole areas of life's proscriptions for the male have to be reversed. He has to be the one provided for rather than the "provider." Perhaps this is the reason so many fail to understand Paul's teachings and Jesus as the Bridegroom.

continuation of the allusion to items which harbor a sweet smell. The comparison, in combination with a vineyard, is most significant, even without the reference to Engedi. A vineyard means stability.

The Hebrews were told to occupy the land and stay there and plant vineyards. Naboth's coveted vineyard associated vineyards with the highest form of ownership. The vineyard and Naboth were linked. The vineyard theme is used by Jesus in His teaching about the vine and branches. Solomon's choice of words is not random. He places Jesus in an appealing setting through the Shulamite's comparison. He is pleasant like the sweet smell of the camphire bush in the midst of a vineyard.

The Shepherd-King's person is distinctive. He flourishes in the stability of His surroundings. He is private to the Shulamite, both in choice and place. He is connected to Engedi. Why this particular location? Engedi was one of the places given to Judah in the distribution of lands (Josh. 15:32). Engedi was the hiding place of the soon coming King (David). Here, David spoke of "not touching God's anointed." He was more willing to wait in Engedi, until the fullness of time, than assert himself. Engedi was the place Saul actually acknowledged the kingship of the one yet to be crowned (I Sam 23). Once called the "pruning of the Palm tree," Engedi maintains its status as the place where all the other interests of the Shulamite are pruned away in love. This pruning is necessary so the righteous-ness of Her life can flourish. (Psalms 92:12 says "the righteous flourish like the palm tree."

Engedi has two other matters of significance to be considered. Israel's enemy was driven out from Engedi by the power of God (2 Chron. 20:2ff). We learn that through the sweet person of Jesus' Being, He drives out the enemies of our lives through His power and His love.

Ezekiel 47 records another facet of the importance of Engedi. Speaking about the river of God which flows from the throne of God, Ezekiel portrays the fishermen of Engedi as those who fish in the living waters and find the fish. This river is also the river of Revelation 22. This river has life in it. All that it touches lives. Jesus said out of the believers' belly would flow rivers of "living water." We become the fishers in the river of love which flows from the throne of God to every part of this earth. We find our fish, and they are endowed with fresh life.

Hold this camphire close to your breast until Jesus' scent permeates the air and leaves its fragrance on your body. Let Him talk to you through the night until you want to hear no other voice. Let Him prune away the dross, drive out the enemies, and teach you the secrets of that which flows only from Him. Learn to love Him in return, and appreciate His loving care. Learn from Him until you are beautifully filled with every ingredient He calls precious. Your Song will change!

"...THOU ART FAIR...THOU HAST DOVES' EYES."
(SONG 1:15,KJV)

Believe me; when you enter into this new relationship with Jesus, you are going to hear something from Him. He doubles His declaration. "Behold" is used twice to emphasize its importance. Because He can speak no lie, whether the fact is relegated, it is true: THOU ART FAIR. Appropriations such as these are similar to other descriptions of a Bride: "without spot or wrinkle."

The Shepherd's comparison for her is: "thou hast doves' eyes." Singleness of vision is one outstanding characteristic of the dove, not the double vision spoken of in James, associated with the double minded man, but single in purpose and sight. The dove, like the eagle, has biblical symbolism. They both possess single vision. Both look across their beaks and see one object, unlike the majority of birds who must turn their heads from side to side. Certainly our thoughts turn to the Spirit who came down in the form of a dove at Jesus' baptism. Naturally, it was a dove sent out by Noah to check for safety. The dove's quiet manner is juxtaposed to the eagle's power and force. The Shulamite has changed; she is both dove and eagle!

The Shulamite has turned away from the cares of the world to envision only her loved one. Her heart is not double minded but singly fixed upon the Shepherd-King. Her manner was brusk in the first of this Chapter, but, like the dove, she is quiet in spirit now. This attribute is most important to Jesus. Examine why Solomon uses this simile, and you will find a key. The dove in the Bible is always _sent_. Could it be that the dove represents the spirit in man that is willing to fly at the command of its possessor and carry out its task with humble power? Jesus had dove's eyes. Humbly, Jesus went about at the command of the Father and fixed His gaze only upon Him. The dove represents the embodiment of the Spirit. To have the Spirit's eyes is to see like the Spirit. No other vision will do for the believer; we must see as the Spirit sees. This is what Paul said in 2 Corinthians 5:14ff:

> "For the love of Christ controls and urges and impels us, because we are of the opinion and conviction that (if) One died for all, then all died: And He died for all, so that all those who live might live no longer to and for themselves, but to and for Him Who died and was raised again for their sake. Consequently, from now on we estimate and regard no one from a (purely) human point of view—in terms of natural standards of value. (No) even though we once did estimate Christ from a human viewpoint and as a man, yet now (we have such knowledge of Him that) we know Him no longer (in terms of the flesh). Therefore if any person is (ingrafted) in Christ, the Messiah, he is (a new creature altogether,) a new creation; the old (previous moral and spiritual condition) has passed away. **Behold,** the fresh and new has come! (Amplified Bible)

Judging from Paul's writing, it is through this process of the new birth that we are brought into harmony with God. Truly, a process is begun when the understanding is opened to realize that the believer possesses the "mind of Christ." To come to terms with this reality may take years for the individual to embrace, but it must be embraced. The message of the Song is the bringing of the Bride into harmony with Jesus. Harmony grows within its pages and is found in this episode.

"...THOU ART FAIR, MY BELOVED,...(SONG 1:16,KJV)"

Like birds calling to one another in the Springtime, the Shulamite hardly hears the Shepherd's accolade before she responds with verse 16. She calls Him "fair." She addresses Him as her "beloved." In verse 13, He is the "well-beloved." Get used to this term of endearment from her, for throughout the Song, it is prevalent.

The Shulamite is a real woman; she is interested in the Shepherd-King, and she is interested in her surroundings. Aesthetics mean much to her. Comfortable and beautiful appointments are appealing to her senses. In this respect, she is still sensual and apparently on a different level in her thinking than the Shepherd is. He does not chide her for what she says. Jesus has a way of taking us where we are in our love for Him and working from there to a higher level. His patience is reflective of His position spiritually. Nonetheless, the Shulamite says: "also our bed is green. The beams of our house are cedar, and our rafters of fir."

Why would these facts be interjected into the lofty conversation the lovers have been having? I believe the Shulamite is expressing the first rays of "oneness" with her love. "Our" is plural possessive. She is pleased with their togetherness in a place as beautiful as could have been imagined. "Our bed is green" has two meanings: righteousness and life. (Perhaps this is why David chose green pastures.) Green is the characteristic of life. One tests a branch or limb to see if it is green, therefore alive. Green is synonymous with growing. The love area where Jesus abides is alive, and growing, and undefiled.

The Shulamite's reference to cedar and fir stirs different meanings. Cedar is a wood notorious for being impervious to rot and insects. Its use in the temple was specified not only for its beauty but also for its personality. Fir wood is a good building material because of its resolute straightness. Other woods have stronger qualities, but none possesses the character of fir. If we abide with Jesus, our surroundings are beautiful, impenetrable to decay and loss, and dependably straight.

Be sensitive to Jesus, to your surroundings with Him, and to the beauty of His provision. Become one with Him. Speak to Him in terms of "our" and "we." On this earth, we must become familiar with His sense of reality and recognize that His is the only reality. We must come into harmony with Him.

CHAPTER FIVE

THE BANQUET HALL

"He brought me to the banqueting house,..."(Song 2:4,KJV)

Because the banquet scene dominates this chapter, I have entitled Chapter Five accordingly. The opening verses, however, act as a shift in tone between the two lovers. Distance between them lessens as they express their feeling about each other. Familiarity draws them closer, not only physically, but orally. Notice the similarity of their phrases and their choice of similes. The reader senses that the atmosphere is charged and these first lines of chapter two are leading into passion, emotion, and commitment. The banquet room is silently waiting for their presence. When they arrive, the spiritual fireworks will start. This room of provision has been prepared for just this time and maturity. The banquet house is the climax point for these opening lines and the door for what will follow. Now observe Solomon, in verse one, as he assumes a more masterful role. No longer do we hear the voice of a Shepherd Boy, but a voice more like a King.

"...THE ROSE OF SHARON,..." (SONG 2:1,KJV)

Standing like the Shulamite in her opening of Chapter 1, Solomon (Jesus) positions Himself at center stage. Pronouncing, "I AM the Rose of Sharon, and the lily of the valley," He rises above the meager "thou are fair" pronouncement of the Shulamite. He is the answer to Isaiah 65:9-10:

> "And I will bring forth a seed out of Jacob, and out of Judah an inheritor of my mountains: and mine elect shall inherit it and my servants shall dwell there. And Sharon shall be a fold of flocks, and the valley of Achor a place for the herds to lie down in, for my people that have sought me."(KJV)

Isaiah, in 33:9, prophesied Sharon to be a wilderness, but now it is seen as a lush place where sheep can dwell. What has made the difference? That seed of Jacob (Jesus), that one out of Judah (Jesus), the "I AM," made the difference. He identifies Himself in the manner of God speaking to Moses and pronounces that He is the bloom of Sharon and Achor. Typically, the passage in Isaiah 65 is attributed to the Gentiles. Considering the Song, the Isaiah passage can be viewed as a combination of the born again, both Jew and Gentile. The Bride is made up of Gentiles as well as born again believers of Israel. Because Israel forgot Her God, desolation has enshrouded the mountain and the valley. When Jesus comes, the deserted places begin to bloom. He is the Rose of Sharon and the lily of the valley. He is the restorer!

Sharing His place of honor is the Shulamite. Jesus declares she is also a lily, "The lily among the thorns." She stands out in the presence of that which is tangled, difficult, and ugly. The bride of Jesus stands out in a world which is awash with thistles, thorny problems. Thorny places seek to choke out the seed of the Word but can not choke out the chosen! Hosea prophesied in 14:5ff:

> "I will heal their backsliding, I will love them freely: for mine anger is turned away from him. I will be as the dew unto Israel: he shall grow as the lily, and cast forth his roots as Lebanon. His branches shall spread, and his beauty shall be as the olive tree, and his smell as Lebanon. They that DWELL under his SHADOW shall return; they shall revive as the corn, and grow as the vine; the scent thereof shall be as the wine of Lebanon. Ephraim shall say, 'What have I to do anymore with idols? I have heard him, and observed him: I am like a green fir tree.'" (KJV)

Just as Jesus is the answer to Hosea's prophecy, so the Shulamite is the answer to Isaiah's. They stand as a complement to one another. Each in his own beauty but each in his rightful place, they are one.

"AS THE APPLE TREE..." (Song 2:3, KJV)

"As the apple tree among the trees of the wood, so is my beloved among the sons," is the Shulamite's reply. In the same genre as the Shepherd-King's compliment of her, she speaks about His rarity. Fruit producing, eye appealing, and nourishing is the fruit of the apple tree. However, I believe what the Shulamite is relating lies more in the setting than the actual tree. She was compared to a lily among the thorns, and He is compared to a tree which blooms into fruit. Its blooms set it apart in beauty during the Spring season. Such a tree is resplendent against the plainer counterparts which surround it. Jesus is outstanding among the sons of men. He is as clearly distinct in His entirety as the apple among the other trees. The tree analogy continues in verse 3, "I sat down under His shadow." Psalms 91:1 says:

> "He that dwelleth in the secret place of the most High shall abide under the shadow of the Almighty." (KJV)

The Bride does dwell in the secret place of the most High! She enjoys a privileged position being face to face with Him. Her unique position with Him affords her entrance to the banquet room. Each advance she makes is an advance toward Him. She is coming closer to what she must become to reign with Him.

Living where God dwells was a rare occurrence in the ancient past. Men like Adam lived there, so did Enoch. Thank God such rarity is not the case with those who chamber with Jesus. The secret place is available to the Bride through the Holy Spirit. Unlike Esther, she is welcomed by Jesus anytime. To dwell in His presence is a quality decision for the believer. It is an act of the will. The believer must make a choice to dwell in that secret place. David made that choice and dwelt in the secret place. Once having experienced that secret place with God, he declares that there is no other place like it. Nothing man can experience comes close in comparison to dwelling under the shadow of His wings. (The secret place could mean dwelling under the Cherubim wings of the inner court of the tabernacle, but it could also mean the prayer closet. Winged coverings are in both places.) The Shulamite sits down under His protection and love with great delight. She relishes being in His presence. She has accepted His invitation and desires to continue there.

"...HIS FRUIT WAS SWEET TO MY TASTE." (SONG 2:3, KJV)

The Shulamite eats of the Shepherd-King's sweet fruit. "His fruit was sweet to my taste," is her affirmation. Unlike the forbidden fruit which cast the world into darkness, she eats freely of the provision found in Him. Never again will this "darling of Jesus" hesitate in approaching Him. (Much has transpired since her first awkward encounter with Him). She is at ease with Him now and greatly loves being in His presence. Taste is soon to be magnified as she enters the banquet room but for now, she has "tasted of the Lord," and He is good (Psalms 34:8). (Explode this thought about taste. Look at the prophets who were commanded to eat the word, to digest it, and consume it, with their inner man.) Review the passages of invitation in I Peter 2:3ff:

> "Since you have already tasted the goodness and kindness of the Lord. Come to Him.... To you then who believe— who adhere to, trust in and rely on Him—is the preciousness;.... Once you were not a people (at all), but now you are God's people; once your were unpitied, but now you are pitied andhave received mercy."
> (Parts of I Peter 2: 3,4,7,10 Amplified Version)

Tasting of His fruit opens to us the power of His Spirit. The fruit of His Spirit in II Peter 1, and the manifestations of those fruit in I Corinthians 12, must be consumed in our inner Being. The fruit of the Spirit indeed is palatable. Galatians 5:22 enumerates that "the fruit of the Spirit is LOVE, joy, peace, longsuffering, gentleness, goodness, faith, meekness, temperance: against such there is no law." Unlike the "roll" of Ezekiel which was sweet to the taste and bitter to his stomach, the Shulamite's taste finds pleasure unspeakable. We also must taste of His fruits, for they are foreign to our flesh but nourishment to our spirit.

Satan has continuously sought to seat us at his table, but those who are the Bride refuse to be seated or to eat (I Cor. 10:21). We eat at the Lord's table, and it is to His table the Shulamite is to be ushered. Here she will really taste of His fruits but not without consequence. Tasting His fruits carries a commitment as discovered in Hebrews 6:4ff:

> "For it is impossible to (to restore and bring to repentance) those who have been once for all enlightened, who have consciously tasted the heavenly gift, and become sharers of the Holy

Spirit, and have felt how good the Word of God is and the mighty powers of the age and world to come, if they deviate from the faith and turn away from their allegiance; (it is impossible) to bring them back to repentance..."   (Amplified Version)

Surely after reading of the propensity involved in tasting of the Lord and His fruit, we are prepared to enter with the Shulamite to the banquet prepared.

"HE BROUGHT ME TO THE BANQUETING HOUSE,..."
(Song 2:4, KJV)

Jesus takes the lead in introducing the Bride to the banquet house. Like a joyous host who wishes to entertain His guests, He has made personal preparation for her. Chapter 2 of this book changes the scene and with it the intensity of love. Often referred to as the house of wine, it is named here the banquet chamber. Keep in mind the Shulamite is about to enter a phase in the relationship which will take her higher. Her interaction with the King has been mostly verbal and contains some social distance in the past verses. Things are about to change, no more social distance! A simple study beginning with the "b" part of this verse will document my conclusion.

"His banner over me was love," is more than a children's song. If you will study similar passages in Song 2:16, 6:3, and 7:10, you will notice a progression in maturity is established by these pronouncements. As the Shulamite's life with the Shepherd-King progresses, so does her level of understanding. At the beginning, she is like a young girl enthralled with her initial entry into real love. Romance is in the air, and the atmosphere of the banquet hall is charged with passion and release. Graces, decorum, and some sensual aspects are integral to the scene. Later in her walk with Him, these aspects fall away into a different kind of love. Here she is closeted away with Him in the privacy of a love nest, but soon she will walk with Him openly in the villages and reign with Him in marriage.

What is considered precious and worth remembering in the banquet hall will soon be secondary. Deeper revelation of the Shepherd-King will continually challenge the Shulamite to step up higher to a new level of interaction with Him. Her life will never be the same after the banquet hall; from here He will usher her into His world. When she opens the door to the banquet hall, she is at the same time closing the door to her former life. She desires to be forever linked to Him. Please know He also desires to be forever linked to her. The tasting of Him she has done before will intensify.

Enter now the banquet hall; experience its exotic smells, its beautiful decor, its transcendent atmosphere. The Shepherd-King and the Shulamite are aware the room holds only the two of them. Never before has she experienced anything like this splendor. A poor Shepherdess enters a King's Palace. Before her is prepared every conceivable delicacy. A King of vast wealth has spared nothing! Breathlessly, she surveys her surroundings. Her wonderment is apparent in her speech and her actions.

Lying before the Shulamite is a display of wealth so vast it would take her many days just to number the dishes. If we could envision the Shepherd-King's demeanor at this point, no doubt a smile would be on His face. How pleased He is to have her here. In one fell sweep she faces the reality of His station, her participation in it, and the preciousness of His provision. He has prepared this for her. Imagine that! He took the time, the effort, the special touches needed to make every provision personal to her. He did not fail. It will be His delight to illumine her as to every aspect of the banquet hall's significance. His delight will be to walk beside her and lovingly interact with her in every discovery. He will point out areas which may have been missed at first glance. He will lay emphasis on some items which she might have overlooked in her naivete. Education is as important in the banquet house as its finery and luxuriant display.

Perhaps you have taken exception to the dramatic license expressed in the former paragraphs. Take note of the facts which the scripture relates in detail. First, the banquet house is a place of the King's preparation (v.4). Second, it is designed for a more intimate time between the two (v.6). Third, the banquet house is of such emotional intensity, the Shulamite has to rest after a time there (v.7). Fourth, in it she declares she is "love sick," which is a change in attitude (v.5). Fifth, the banquet hall is a place she wishes to stay cloistered with Him (v.10). Last, the declaration of "His banner over me *was* love" is made here (v.4). Note the word "was" is italicized. Although it was introduced to the text for clarity by the translators, delete it and see the change it makes. Read it without the italic as a declaration to the power of Love, "His banner over me: LOVE."

Before further investigation as to the interior of the banquet house, let us examine the passage about the "banner of love." If you will study the tabernacle of Moses, you will discover there were banners, or flags, flying from each corner of the "tent of meeting." On each banner was a different animal or figure: the face of a lion, ox, eagle, and man. These banners represented the creation of God. (Their further symbolism would make another study and is significant as to their several attributes. That the banners were flying is sufficient for this study). The banner flying over this tent of meeting had one word emblazoned on it: LOVE. Whereas God the Father met man as Creator in the tent of meeting, Jesus meets His bride under different circumstances in the banquet hall. The glory of God hovered <u>over</u> the tabernacle, but the presence of God dwells <u>in</u> the banquet house. God revealed Himself in cloud and fire over the tabernacle; Jesus reveals Himself as a man in the vulnerability of a room. Cloven tongues of Pentecost with a rushing wind, give way to a lover's embrace beneath the gentle flapping of the banner of LOVE. Faith has come to fruition. Things hoped for are now real. God's Son is meeting man in a way deemed impossible before Calvary. No wonder the flags are flying! Yet, there is more.

Another close parallel is the custom of the King to fly a heralding banner over the palace when He was present. The sight of the banner flying with royal emblem was a comfort to all who dwelt in the holy city. A banner of LOVE flying over the banquet house is a sign the King is present. The emblazoned emblem, gently flapping in the breeze, is a joy to the daughters of Jerusalem and to all who love the King. Yet, there is more!

The King's invitation to each potential member of the "bride of Christ" to enter the banquet house is still open. In this facility of His design, the bride will learn what is important to Him and what belongs to her. Imagine being ushered into a panoramic production on which each screen flashes scenes of the finished promises of God. Each interval would introduce a wealth of reality which would illumine the passages of the Word. Miracles promised by Jesus would be portrayed with you as a central figure. Holy Spirit-led occurrences throughout your life would find dramatic reality in fulfillment of "being led by the Spirit." Great promises and illustrations of the Word would permeate the room. Provision of every nature would be dramatized before you. Meticulous detail would stand out in vivid awareness as your mind and heart sought to fathom its wonder. From time to time you would ask that the action stop. You would turn to Him and say "just hold me." "With His left hand under my head, and with his right hand He embraces me" (v. 6). Soft tears spill over ever gladdened eyes as the reality of His provision is replayed in your memory. Pauline utterances would flow from your lips, "O the depth of the riches both of the wisdom and knowledge of God!" (Romans 11:33).

> "That he would grant you, according to the riches of His glory, to be strengthened with might by his Spirit in the inner man; that Christ may dwell in your hearts by faith; that ye, being rooted and grounded in love, may be able to comprehend with all saints what is the breadth, and length, and depth, and height; and to know the love of Christ, which passeth knowledge, that ye might be filled with all the fullness of God. Now unto him that is able to do exceeding abundantly above all that we ask or think, according to the power that worketh in us, unto him be glory in the church by Christ Jesus throughout all ages, world without end. Amen." (Ephesians 3:16-21 KJV)

Assurances are whispered into trembling ears as scripture upon scripture is revealed. Little verses are projected on the "mind screen"; little verses thought insignificant bloom before you. Laughter breaks out between the two in the banquet hall as she exclaims, "How could I have been so blind as not to see that!" He holds her close, and she knows from His touch that everything is "all right." The daughters of Jerusalem linger close to the banquet house, listening to the banter and love making. They are instructed by the bride not to enter the scene or "stir up" or invoke further his love in her until He so desires. They are to monitor this task based on His discretion. (We are told to "stir up the gift of God within us"; she wants no stirring unless He directs it.)

"STAY ME WITH FLAGONS, COMFORT ME..."
(SONG 2:5 KJV)

The King is aware of the vastness of all the Shulamite has been expected to comprehend and forgives her inability to continue. Her emotions have been tested; her ability to contain has been strained, but her joy has found new levels in Him. The Shulamite has spoken to Him her inmost heart, and He knows well it is pure and good. "Stay me with flagons" means "satisfy me with raisin cakes or the wine cakes" in some translations. "Satisfy me with what I once sought to satisfy you with," might be a good translation. The apple reference, "comfort me with apples," is about Him. She has already declared He is like the apple tree in verse 3, so she continues the analogy. "Your presence is enough" would be a good understanding of this verse. In other words, "I am satisfied with raisin cakes and your presence – that would be all I desire." (The poets have said of lovers: "a loaf of bread, a glass of wine, and Thou.") Yet, there is more!

No, the provision of God is not diminished by our inability to grasp all He has for us in one sitting or a thousand. A million sermons could not accomplish in us what one whisper from Him can accomplish. He speaks to us through His Word (the Bible), and often our responses are meager before the vastness of His promise. We are satisfied with wine-cakes and His presence! (An interesting study in Hosea reveals a hidden relevance to the wine cake. Hosea 3:1-5 begins with wine cake offered to other gods with significance to a straying bride. Hosea prophesies that Israel will repent and turn away from adultery and offering these items to strange gods and will seek the right things and the true God in the end time.)

Jesus is not satisfied with wine cakes. Wine cake love offerings make fine tokens to strange gods, but faith is what turns Him on. He desires our faith to grow until His faith and power flow freely through us. He who gave the promises also lived the promises! We must live them too! Living out these affirmations by faith involves stepping outside our comfort zones. Someday the banquet house will give way to the treasure house (Chapter 7). The Bride has some maturing to do.

Naturally, the Shulamite's desire is to remain in the room of provision. She feels safe here and is unchallenged by the demands of life. The King reigns; she rests. We are told to rest in Him, but rest is not retirement. So, her reverie is broken by the sound of the King's voice. Time is up! She clamors at his entrance. The thing to note is that He does not reenter the banquet house. He stands outside looking in and offers her the first of many invitations to join him.

"...RISE UP, MY LOVE, MY FAIR ONE, AND COME AWAY." SONG (2:10KJV)

Juxtapose the responses of the two at this moment, and you will notice different viewpoints. The Shulamite's response to the King's voice is on the same level as the banquet house. She is desperately in love with Him, is happy to have Him close at hand. "The voice of my beloved! behold, he cometh leaping upon the mountains, skipping upon the hills," is so written to show the upbeat and airy enthusiasm of their relationship. Repeatedly in the Song, reference is made to the "voice of the beloved." Before this book ends, you will know the significance of the reference to His voice. The Bride thinks she knows Him now; but in the end, she will declare "make me to hear your voice." Jesus' voice is the rallying point of His sheep. In teaching His disciples, He underscores the necessity of knowing His voice: "My sheep know my voice." In the last verses of the Song, we will discover the importance of hearing His voice. For now, let the phrase dwell quietly within our frame of reference. Turn your attention to her reaction to His voice.

Youthful verve is in the Shulamite's voice. She likens the Shepherd-King to a "roe" or "young deer." She is overjoyed at the vitality He displays. He is the embodiment of energy. Her lover returns in strength and beauty. No doubt her mind is racing with thoughts of continued revelry and greater joys of being together. Imagine her astonishment to hear Him ask her to leave her place of love and rest.

Just such shock comes to the church! Dwelling in the comfort of the promises of God, insulated from the vulgarities of daily trial, munching wine cake called "communion," the temptation to grow fatter is more tempting than obeying His invitation. "What! Enter the world outside to follow You; why wouldn't it be better to stay here and learn some more?" is often the reply.

Could this be the reason God gave Moses instructions to build a tent? The tent of meeting was portable and designed to move to other levels of commitment. The Jerusalem temple stabilized a nomadic, wandering people and gave an urban place to the Jews. That is why Jesus told the woman at the well the time would come when people would not worship God either in the Temple or on that mountain. The temple at Jerusalem had become a banquet hall, and its purpose was lost. Jesus' words to the Samaritan woman were not cryptic; they were true. The day has come when those who worship Him will not worship on mountains or in temples. They will worship Him in Spirit and in Truth. His invitation is to leave the predictable and enter a walk of faith (dependency on Him).

"...THE WINTER IS PAST,..." (SONG 2:11 KJV)

The King has given time for the Shulamite to recoup. She has had ample time to absorb His assurances of staying beside her. Time has been spent in His arms while hearing His pronouncements of unconditional love. These kinds of moments are necessary; they are designed to deepen commitment and give assurances. The banquet halls' importance is dignified by His provision in it but not to the point of reluctance to leave it. The Shulamite will soon learn the importance of being alongside Him. She will rue the day she did not take this first invitation. She will experience trials never intended for her because of her hesitancy. Although it is good to be in cloister with the Master, it is better to have His smile while walking the road with Him. (The disciples were taught as they walked with Him. Every encounter along the way with Him brought deeper foundations to their personal conviction. Rarely did He bring them to a house; often He brought them to the hillside. For further teachings about the lessons of the banquet house, read Addendum I.) Notice where He is standing. He is standing on the outside looking in. (Could this be the place where Jesus has to stand to address the Church?)

The Shulamite sees the King standing behind *their* (our) wall. Ownership is gaining a foothold in her mindset. More and more you will hear her utter the personal possessive pronoun "our." "His" and "hers" is becoming "ours." Such is the way of blending in life. It is their wall, their window, their lattice outside. Here He stands calling, "Come away." Always in the most endearing tones, loving her with greater intensity, He calls.

Notice the reasons the King gives to the Shulamite for leaving with Him now. First, the harshness of winter is past. (It will be easier to travel, fewer weather delays, and more amicable conditions.) Second, the rain is over and gone. (If the outpouring of the Holy Spirit is equated with rain, then this means, "You are enabled and equipped to make this journey." The outpouring has already happened.)

If eschatological timetables can be applied in these verses, this is the wonderful "end-time." If not, it is still a marvelous period. Just being with the King, viewing the world with Him, seeing what makes Him enthusiastic, is enough. Spring brings refreshing. This is the time of refreshing! Flowers bloom and beckon which calls for a lighthearted response. Hear Him cite the singing of birds and the voice of the turtledove as evidences the season has changed. He plies the Shulamite by pointing to the green figs and the tender grape as further evidence. (Jesus often equated historical change to seasonal changes. He told the disciples they would know the latter days by evidence just like these.)

A few items in the King's "list of Spring" have greater significance than others. He mentions the turtledove. The turtledove could be used (instead of a lamb) as an offering for sin and cleansing. He says, "the fig tree putteth forth her green figs. (The fig tree was cursed for not having fruit when Jesus passed by, even when its time was not ready.) He speaks of the smell of the vine and the tender grapes. (The vine and its fruit will be discussed later.) The flowers of the field have been pointed to as being better arrayed than Solomon in all His glory. Taken together, a wide range of meaning can be garnered. Put them all together and this is the meaning, "The outpouring of the Holy Spirit (rain) has showered down upon the cleansed ones (turtledove-people) whose fruit (fig) is yielded to Him. The bride in such condition is arrayed with the provision of Jesus (flowers/lilies) which is better than the kings of the earth."

"...THE VOICE OF THE TURTLE IS HEARD IN OUR LAND;" (SONG 2:12,KJV)

Jesus takes to himself the plural possessive form in v.12. "Our land" means He possesses nothing without the Bride. Jointly they rule and reign, although she has not yet come to such a position within herself; He is calling that which is not as though it was. He constantly draws her, requiring deeper commitment and greater faith. Reference to the tender grapes is an opening for a teaching about little foxes spoiling the vines in verse 15.

"ARISE, MY LOVE, MY FAIR ONE, AND COME AWAY." (SONG 2:13,KJV)

"Arise my love, my fair one, and come away," is spoken <u>outside</u> the wall of the house of banqueting. It is accompanied by the same ardor as a lover who longs to have his love beside Him. Jesus spoke to His disciples in similar turn, "take my yoke upon you and LEARN of me."(Matt. 11:29) To learn of Him requires walking, talking, bearing His burdens, and living with Him. Feeling His pain, experiencing His ways of doing and being, all the while being a constant companion, is His method of instruction. Those who accompanied Him to a mountain top and had fellowship with Moses and Elijah heard the same appeal as the Shulamite. Their combined voices to persuade Him to remain and build three tabernacles could not drown out the pitiful cry of a child below. Hurriedly, they went to the rescue of the other disciples, and He cast the demon out. Citing prayer and fasting as the vehicle for the cure, the disciples quickly understood He had no time for lingering in stodgy temples when a mission field was below. "Come away" will be heard again in the Song and always used in the same manner.

"...SECRET PLACES OF THE STAIRS,..." (SONG 2:14,KJV)

"O my dove, in the cleft of the rock, in the secret places of the stairs" is an appropriate response for the person not sure of an invitation. The "O my dove," is an endearment in keeping with their love talk. If you appropriate the dove symbolism to this statement, the element of "degree in kind" takes shape. "Since I am your dove," paraphrasing the Shulamite, "you are my dove, but you dwell at a higher level than I do." "You are inviting me to come away with you to a place I am not ready to attain. You dwell in the high places of the rock, in the unknown areas of the steep places. You are inviting me to the unknown and the unexplored. You are asking me to reach a level beyond my capability. I am content to hear your sweet voice, just to look on your face. Besides, there are areas of my life I need to work on before I am able to accompany you. There are little foxes that seek to take away the life-giving blessings you are imparting to me. We can overcome these little foxes; we can take them out of my life, but now I am just a beginner. The little grapes are just now coming forth. O my dove, understand my heart belongs to you, I know how you want me to grow and understand, but give me more time. I accept your love and kisses; I want more of you. I want you to continue having faith in me, but don't ask me to go forth too quickly. You continue to feed among (us). We are the lilies (those in the thorn patches of life). You are aware of my need to have more assurance. Please stay the night until the day breaks and teach me more and surely by then I will be able to follow. Until the shadows of fear vanish, until I can have your confidence and be as the deer or the roe is all I ask. O my beloved, bound over these mountains of uncertainty and fear that separate us."

You may need to re-read this paraphrase. It is an attempt to incorporate a feeling tone as well as the underlying teaching. The Shulamite's love for the King is great but not to a point of following Him into the unknown. (If you will look ahead, you will discover her hesitancy is manifested in other places.)

Chapter 3 opens with them separated. She is in her bed chamber, and the King is absent. Evidently, she did not take His invitation to "come away with me." Just as Christians exercise their will, so the Shulamite exercises hers. Jesus never violates the gift of will within the individual. However, it does not change his invitation to "come away with me." Her rationale in not following Him is based on self-analysis. This is a deadly form of unbelief. To determine one is not ready, based on finite reason, is heaven's treason. His love and grace covered her and protected her through this ordeal, but the reader must realize it opened the door to unbelief, loss of time with Him, and retarded the time of their union.

In later chapters, much will hinge on this decision to delay following the King immediately. (Philip in the New Testament understood the lesson of this Song. When the Holy Spirit spoke to him about going to the Eunuch, he did not hesitate; he did not take pains to assure his wife, his children, or pack his bag. The Bible records the necessity of his immediate response. It chronicles His journey so their paths would juncture, and the will of the Father would be accomplished. Philip did not take regard to time frames or travel distances. He offered no hesitancy but immediately went to the task. Underlying this action is a profound truth: God never says "go" without total provision for the "go-er." He will take care of costs, provide the travel arrangements, and care for those areas of responsibility left behind. This is a truth the Shulamite and the Church must hold sacred.)

"O MY DOVE,..." (SONG 2:14)

A dove in the clefts of rock sounds out of place. Eagles dwell in clefts and occupy the steep places. Perhaps to the Shulamite the high places of God seemed inaccessible. Her judgment of their range may have been as distorted as her self-analysis. She is not above being wrong in her appraisals; recount her opening lines about being undesirable. She is correct in one aspect: the King does dwell in the high places. The word "stairs" used in the passage means steep. There are other Bible references to such places:

> "The Lord is my light and my salvation; whom shall I fear or dread? The Lord is the refuge and stronghold of my life; of whom shall I be afraid? When the wicked, even my enemies and my foes, came upon me to eat up my flesh, they stumbled and fell. Though a host encamp against me, my heart shall not fear; though war arise against me, (even then) in this will I be confident. One thing have I asked of the Lord, that will I seek after, inquire for and insistently require, that I may dwell in the house of the Lord (in His presence) all the days of my life, to behold and gaze upon the beauty (the sweet attractiveness and the delightful loveliness) of the Lord, and to meditate, consider and inquire in His temple. For in the day of trouble He will hide me in His shelter; IN THE SECRET

PLACE OF HIS TENT WILL HE HIDE ME; HE WILL SET ME HIGH UPON A ROCK."
(Psalms 27:1-5 Amplified Version)

This Psalm has most of the elements found in the Song passage. It does not have the fear, unbelief, and salient attitude of the Shulamite as to not being worthy of the high places. The Psalmist portrays confidence that, no matter what the circumstances, the Lord will provide. He reiterates the Lord dwells in the high places, and he will be taken to those places with Him. He recognizes to have the presence of the Lord, you must trust the Lord. The Shulamite may have wanted the presence of the Lord without the climb.

"...LET ME SEE...LET ME HEAR..." (SONG 2:14, KJV)

Countenance and voice are now the focus of the Shulamite's desire. The eye-gate and the ear-gate are turned toward the King. She cries, "Let me see your countenance and let me hear your voice." These two requests are heard again in Chapter 8:13-14. To those who experience Jesus, these are the two most common cries.

Moses sought God's face as well as His voice. David declared his greatest desire was to behold His countenance. Simeon desired enough life to see baby Jesus' face. His countenance generates glory. His voice calms the storms of life and calls us to peace and safety. The Bride will soon learn in the end time, this will be her greatest desire.

Throughout the Song there is reference to the "voice" of the beloved. Twice in this chapter reference is made to His voice. Any student of the Word flashes back to when Jesus said, "My sheep hear my voice, and I know them, and they follow me (John 10:27)." In Song 2:8 is the voice that alarms. The King's voice awakens the Shulamite and signals His coming. Such a voice the world will hear in the last day. The voice of 2:14 is the voice of intimacy. Paraphrased, it might read, "I love to hear your voice." Brideship must have this ingredient. To see His countenance is more than His face. It is His total being when you are with Him. Countenance speaks to smiles, frowns, demeanor, attitude, and body language. He is delighted when she is near Him. She feels this **delight**.

She wants to have His responses to her. This is not some Greek god in the sky. He is a lover with arms, personality, and possessiveness. Hearing His voice is calming to her fears. Hearing His voice signals a response from Him. He talks to her. He builds faith within her. His voice is Him. (Study the voice of God throughout the Word.) His faith is projected in His voice. No lie courses His lips. His voice is creative and renewing.

"...THY COUNTENANCE IS COMELY." (SONG 2:14,KJV)

"Sweet is thy voice and thy countenance is comely," reflect more than love-banter. David spoke of the beauty of the Lord. We know at His right- hand are pleasures forevermore. His countenance truly is comely. When His presence outweighs our schedule, and His voice supersedes the media, we might just begin to approach brideship.

Relationships require work, interaction, and honesty. The Shulamite is honest. She is transparent to the King. She longs to be like Him, but one thing stands in the way: her self appraisal. She knows her heart is fragile, and her understanding is tender. She knows how Satan wishes to steal what she has in the Shepherd-King and what He has invested in her.

"TAKE US THE FOXES..." (SONG 2:15,KJV)

Reflecting on her spiritual stature, the Shulamite sees foxes among the vines. Knowing the King is the Vine, and she is the branch, becomes apparent in this verse. Life-giving nourishment, pumping new avenues of joy into her being, originates in Him. Tender grapes of understanding are just forming in her person, and she does not wish for them to vanish. Demons of darkness, doubt, and unbelief, seem always to be seeking those tender morsels of His making. To be aware of the foxes' presence is one thing; to make decisions based on their machinations is another. She appraises her situation correctly. She realizes she must take away the foxes. She declares: "Take us the foxes, the little foxes that spoil the vines (2:15)." In other words, "Help me capture and cast out every little desire, deception, and will that would take away your Word. Heal every hurt and broken spot in my heart."

Listen, there is another voice speaking! "Do not concentrate on the foxes and let them keep you from rising higher in Me," might be the unspoken response. (There is a relationship in this verse to a passage in 4:12-5:1. In those verses the Shulamite desires to rid her life of anything displeasing to the King. In those subsequent verses, she invites Him into the garden of her heart to see His will has been accomplished.)

Concentrating on little devils will keep you from responding to Jesus' call to "come away." He does not call you to do what He would judge to be impossible for you. The challenge of His call may catch you seemingly unprepared, but drop your opinion and adopt His.

Others have had similar experiences in the Lord. "The Lord is with thee, Thou mighty man of valor," were words that took Gideon by surprise, but after a slight hesitation, he rose to the occasion (Judges 6:12). Moses hesitated and thought himself unworthy and unskilled for the task of leading the children of Israel; how wrong he was. The great similarity to these three events is simple: all the subjects were alone with the Lord when His invitation came. It is very difficult to weasel when there are only two. Each of their self-appraisals was similar and reflected honesty, which is precisely why the Lord took time and worked with them.

Taking care of foxes is no slight task; in this the Shulamite is to be commended. Truly, it is a task for both the King and the Bride to accomplish as a unit. Foxes are characterized as being sly, conniving, and stealthy. They often enter unbeknown, and their effect is devastating. They are pictured as thieves entering a private vineyard. Tearing, and not consumption, is their major threat. She fears what she has received from Him will be taken away or damaged. The vineyard of the heart is a precious place, and it is where she glories in her progress of faith. Her use of a "vineyard" as a comparative correlates to Jesus' use of the vineyard. It also correlates to her reference about not keeping her own vineyard in Chapter 1. That which she longed for requires effort; she is now the keeper of her vineyard.

It is the Bride's personal responsibility to apprehend the foxes and protect what has been given her. She cannot do it alone. The Holy Spirit must reveal points of entrance, times of destruction, and their intended purpose. Spiritual warfare is part of our territory in the Jesus walk. Something is to be said for faith at this point: We must trust Him with our vineyard! He calls her to "come away," knowing this is best for her. Staying in a place she has grown accustomed to might increase vulnerability to destruction. His invitation to join Him in the high places is primary to her survival. Foxes rarely frequent the high places.

"MY BELOVED IS MINE AND I AM HIS:..." (SONG 2:16,KJV)

The Shulamite is to be commended on this phrase: "My beloved is mine, and I am his: he feedeth among the lilies (Song 2:16)." Similar to the passage in 2:4 (about the banner), this passage reflects a higher level of knowing the King. In 2:4, she acknowledges His superiority and emphasizes His provision. In 2:16, she makes a claim on the person of Jesus. "He is mine" is possessive and exclusive. By making this statement, she opens up new vistas for progression in Him. She acknowledges His desire to be possessed by His Bride, as well as possessing the Bride. In Jesus, we are not only to be possessed of Him, but also He must be possessed by us. This fact is crucial.

Thousands of people, for example, read the Word of God, relish its teachings, and love its words. The real question is how much of it do they own? Because Jesus is the Word made flesh, there is a real analogy made here. When the Shulamite made this statement, she is revealing her theology. To be possessed by the King is to possess Him. He does not love without allowing demand to be put on that love. Because His love is without limit, it is the epitome of I Corinthians 13. No demand placed on it is too great. It never fails to deliver the answer of the appeal made to it. It is unlike earthly, romantic love which consumes the marketplace. Endemic to earthly relationships is a presupposed limit to love. The love Jesus has for His Bride is without limit or parameter. Peter spoke to that supposed limit in his query: "How oft shall I forgive him?" The answer Jesus gave astonished him; it had no limit. The love between the Shulamite and the Shepherd Boy exceeds the boundaries of the human. Hosea exemplified it. Jesus lived it.

"...UPON THE MOUNTAINS OF BETHER." (SONG 2:17, KJV)

In my Chapter II, where the entire story is given as a unit, I handled verse 17 of the Song, Chapter 2 without explanation. My interest was a broad understanding of that Chapter; now it is time to look into each location as it appears in the text. These locations are not randomly chosen. Their significance is often passed over without comprehending their unique contribution to the text. Reference to *Bether* is important because it means "separation." The Shulamite implores the King to turn back to her on the mountains of separation. Whether her concerns were He was getting so far ahead of her they were being separated is speculation. It is good speculation, however. Clearly, she is calling for Him to help her catch up.

"Until the day break" means it has not yet happened; it is still dark. Darkness is often a reference to "ignorance or a state of being unlearned." A call for the dawn and the fleeing of shadows may well have been an appeal for more time. In other words, time to make clear in the Shulamite's thinking all that has transpired. "Let me get my thinking clear," might be a paraphrase. However, answering every question, clearing up every theological nuance, and inspecting every detail is often counterproductive to progress. Some things are illumined only by faith. Other things only clear up when the Master of the subject matter takes the lead. Along the way He teaches through the difficulties. Be extremely careful at this point. He teaches as both Jesus and His Bride pass through the difficulties inherent to life and those imposed by Satan. An apprenticeship to Jesus is how the disciples learned; why not the Bride? Those who wrote the inspired Word, wrote from a myriad of experiences as they walked and practiced what He taught. It is time for the Bride to "hit the road" and leave the cloistered banquet house!

(Although there is a separation in knowledge and understanding of the mysteries of God between Jesus and His Bride, she finds it is better not to be separated spiritually and physically from Him. His invitation to her is an open-ended one with this import: When the bride decides being with Him is better than being alone—she can "draw near to Him." The Bride, like the church at large, has a will of her own. She must make the decision to join Him. He will not violate her will; He will honor it.)

CHAPTER SIX

PRECIOUS PRESENCE

"I held him, and would not let him go,..." (Song 3:4,KJV)

"BY NIGHT ON MY BED I SOUGHT HIM... I FOUND HIM NOT." (SONG 3:1,KJV)

Troubled sleep and tossing restlessness is often the result of not heeding the call of God. Introspection and chasing foxes trouble the soul. Seeking Him where He is not is fruitless, especially after having relinquished His invitation to: "come away." Isaiah 55:6-7 clearly states:

> "Seek ye the Lord while he may be found, call ye upon him while he is near: let the wicked forsake his way, and the unrighteous man his thoughts: and let him return unto the Lord, and he will have mercy upon him; and to our God, for he will abundantly pardon." (KJV)

The Shulamite, like many after her, awakens to the fact she has eclipsed an opportunity to be by the King's side. She has not accepted His invitation to join Him. Tossing on her bed, she may rationalize her nonacceptance was understandable, but it carries with it no remedy. The only remedy to her situation is to search for Him and find Him. It will be to her dismay that she soon recognizes how difficult a path she has chosen. There is one bit of credit she can claim; she does not linger long on her bed of decision. She concludes she must find Him.

The Shulamite depends on the promise the King made of not being far away, so she determines to search for Him. Realize she could have gone with Him, but she chose to remain. It was her decision. She chose to sleep, and during sleep, her opportunity was gone. (The church asleep is in the same condition.) It is again her will expressed in going after Him. As before, she inquires of Him by quizzing the watchmen, but not to her satis-faction (Notice the plural form of the noun: <u>watchman</u>).

The watchmen know where the King has been, but not where He is. He is not with the watchmen. Let it be stated without reservation; seeking Him where He is not is pointless! Why is this fact so important to comprehend? Many people are doing just that. Multitudes seek for Him in religious experience, mystical tantras, and ecclesiastical strongholds, but He is not there. Rivers of ink and mountains of paper are devoted to the subject of where to find Him but only to the confusion of the reader. Most of the guides point to where He is **not**! If you depend on experience, knowledge, or social interaction to find Jesus, you will be without Him. One of the teachings in this chapter is that those charged with knowing where He is, actually haven't a clue.

Keep in mind it is the Shulamite's decision to search for the King. She seeks Him on her terms. Her territory (her bed at home) is more appealing than His. (The rivers of Abana and Pharpar (II Kings 5:12) may seem better than the prophets' Jordan, but God's healing was not in Abana and Pharpar.) Her bed is more familiar and personal, and here she sought to hold Him based on earthly terms. The stark reality comes to her: "I sought Him, but I found Him not." Could it be men and women crowd pews at 10:00 a.m. Sunday seeking to find Him and, like the Shulamite, leave at 12 Noon having "found Him not?" Incantations are not Him. Creeds and prayers are not Him. Grand music and robed choirs are not Him. Shouting crowds and silent sitters search for Him, but He is not there. He is not in the wind, the fire, or the earthquake, for He is in the still small voice. Towering offerings and cancelled checks cannot buy what must be obtained from this keeper of the oil. (To be a bride one must have the oil.) It comes from the olive being pressed between two lovers holding one another so tightly each drop is precious beyond words. From this oil press comes the substance of faith and the evidence of things not seen. To be without Him is darkness. Her search is in the night. It is night where He is not!

Rousing herself from her bed, the Shulamite goes to the streets in search of the King. I reiterate this fact because of its importance. This event, coupled with one other similar event, will clinch her resolve never to be where He is not again. The city is not a safe place to be at night, especially when you are a woman alone. She will find this out in Chapter 5:7ff. Now, she searches in the obvious places: in the broad ways. How cryptic is her search, for "broad is the way that leadeth to destruction." He is not there!

Two facts are apparent: First, Jesus is not in the old haunts and the worlds' broadway; the other fact is the Shulamite has undergone a change in her person, and the world senses it. Just as it is pointless to obsess over past sins, it is fruitless to search for Him in worldly places. On broadway there may be fine churches and glittering signs, but He is not there. On broadway old friends hang out in reliable order, but if you are searching for Him, they have no idea where He is. Rebuff is in the streets, for you are now changed. Once in His presence, the fragrance of His being is ON you. You are perfumed by His perfume, for being held closely by Him causes this to happen. Simon Peter had that fragrance on him, and cursing denial could not cover it up. You are changed when you have been with Jesus, and the world and broadway know the difference. You look different, your talk is different, your habits are different because you are changed.

Frantically, the Shulamite searches to no avail. Then something happens: "the watchmen that go about the city found me: to whom I said, Saw ye him whom my soul loveth? (3:3)" Who are these watchmen? A good place to start looking for an answer is in the writings of Ezekiel, for he talks about watchmen. Ezekiel recognized the watchmen were spiritual leaders, prophets, priests, and men charged with keeping the faith. God told Ezekiel He made Ezekiel a "watchman to the house of Israel." He gave Ezekiel a mandate to warn Israel of their wicked ways or face the judgment of having their blood on his hands. If he so warned them, the blood of those who heard and did not listen would not be on his hands.

The watchmen, in a practical sense, were charged with keeping the populace of the city safe. Their responsibility was to warn of impending danger. Their duty was to keep a sharp eye out for intruders and interlopers and to maintain peace in the streets. They were charged with the protection of women, children, and the elderly. Watchfulness was to be continued through the night along with alertness to danger. (Jesus teaches the night watch will sound the alarm when the bridegroom comes.) Twice, the watchmen are singled out for observation in this text.

On neither occasion do the watchmen carry out their duty. The Shulamite asks a mute question, "Saw ye, him whom my soul loveth?" They answer nothing.

If the watchmen in society are the spiritual leaders, the clergy, the ecclesiastics, and they are charged with spiritual duties, then what is their duty? They are to warn the people. They are to be alert to dangers. They are to protect the saints and those who are weak and infirm. They are to be vigilant, to sound the alarm early and not fall asleep in the night. Could it be the modern watchmen of our day are posed a mute question: "Saw ye him whom my soul loveth?" Why is there no answer forthcoming? They know where He has been, but not where He is!

Why does Solomon make graphic this scene? Is it not that the Song is about a new order, a new day spiritually? As the New Testament events were a judgment to the watchmen (the Jews) of Jesus' day, the Song is an indictment to the watchmen of the last days (established religion). Having the name "watchman" carries the same judgment as it did in Ezekiel's day. Woe be to the "watchman" who fails his task. Greater judgment falls on the teacher than the student. Ultimately, their dereliction of duty will lead to the onerous scene in Chapter 5 when we see the watchman attack the bride! Such erosion of duty is unacceptable.

Jesus has placed in the watchman's hand a spiritual trust. Alas, it has happened; the trust is violated! Perhaps this is why Jesus admonishes the believer to WATCH and pray. Could it be the responsibility of the believer himself to be his own watchman? (Daniel discovered there were "watchers" in heaven (Daniel 4). They are "watching" over the saints. Jesus wants "watchers" on the earth doing the same thing. These prayer warriors are to "watch" in the Spirit.) Like the Shulamite, the disciples fell asleep during the time Jesus was sweating drops of blood. When Jesus found them asleep, His admonition was a rebuke for not "watching" and praying one hour. Vigilance is the theme of the last days. We know not the time the bridegroom cometh!

"IT WAS BUT A LITTLE THAT I PASSED FROM THEM, BUT I FOUND HIM..." (SONG 3:4, KJV)

Many of those who are searching in the streets of the city today are really the Bride. They are looking for Jesus. They might not appear to be the Bride, but they soon will find Jesus and be the Bride. Streets of all nations are filled with multitudes who need to know Jesus is not far from them. The precise reason He requested the Shulamite to "come away" with Him was to go to these multitudes. Jesus will always be found reaching out to the lost sheep. He is not willing one will perish. The streets are difficult places; they are not friendly to Jesus, but this is where the mission field is and this is where Jesus dwells. When I refer to the streets, I speak not just of those mission ministries for the homeless; I refer to those who are in office buildings, work places, schools, hospitals, nursing homes. I refer to those who occupy places of power, executive suites, and brokerage houses. I refer to those who deliver goods, sail ships, and labor in mills. I refer to the multitudes who form the collage of faces in your everyday life. These well might be the bride. From prisons to college campuses, the teaming cry is still, "Saw ye Him?" Thank God the Song shows the Bride rewarded for her search.

Not far past the watchmen, the Shulamite discovers the King. What a relief! Although it has been just a short time since she has been in His presence, it seems like an eternity. Coming from the "frantic search mode," it is a burden lifted to find Him. She melts into His arms. She puts a grip on Him that will not let Him go. Somewhere there is a lesson here. If she had chosen to go with Him rather than to sleep, she never would have experienced this ordeal.

Thousands of Christians are laboring under the frenzy of finding Jesus. They have lost Him somewhere between a place called "my will" and a place called "complacency." It is not comical to watch the frantic search. Churches having exercised their will instead of following His, have awakened from their sleep and discovered Him gone. In a frantic effort to ameliorate their error, they do frenzied things to get Him back. Programs are launched, committees are formed, and sad as it may sound, they sometimes just try to cover up the fact of His absence. The search goes on.

Those who really search for Jesus find Him. He is not far from any of us, but beware of continued disobedience. Because of her neglect, the Bride will experience much more before this ordeal is finished. Another invitation will come to her, and again she will not respond with a simple, "I will." The next experience is of such magnitude it acts as a turning point in her life. It will take but one more experience to persuade her to accept His call. From that time forward, she will not be out of the sight of the King, and her greatest desire will be to live in His presence.

Having acted on the teaching of Jesus to "seek and ye shall find," she finds Him and brings her lover home. Strangely, she desires to bring Him home to her mother. Is this an indication of some greater decision on her part to be His forever? I believe it is! She wants Him to know she desires a deeper commitment. She wants to be betrothed to Him. She wants Him to be familiar with her family. Betrothing often leads to such behavior. Rebekah (Gen.24:28) went and told her mother's household when it was discovered she was the appointed bride. Bringing Jesus home to the family is a natural order. Just let some family member fall in love with Jesus and observe what happens. Jesus is all he or she can talk about in the presence of family and friends. He or she urges family members to share his or her joy. This individual wants parents to learn of Him and love Him as he or she does. But what is the reaction when one brings a personal Jesus home to a house filled with those who only peripherally know about Him? That is when a person might decide it would have been better to have "come away with Him."

After the Shulamite accomplishes her desire for Him to meet the family, a scene change is in the offing. Now it is her turn to speak to the daughters of Jerusalem. She charges them by the "roes and deer" which look so beautiful in the field. She tells them not to disturb her, not to use their power to stir love. "Do not stir up love, until He pleases," is her admonition. Just as in Chapter 2 verse 7, she now instructs them to take their lead from Him. She is attentive to care for Him. She wants nothing that does not originate from Him to be in her life. (Do you really want to know how to judge a believer or church? Discover how attentive they are to the things of Jesus and how they are protective and jealous over His interests. Precious is His presence to them. Behold how they care for His work, His comfort, His pleasure. Soon you will discover those who do so want nothing in their life that is disruptive to Him.)

"WHO IS THIS THAT COMETH OUT OF THE WILDERNESS...?" (Song 3:6,KJV)

If you ask the reason for the ensuing passages, you will find that they evolve around a theme: "Getting to Know You." The Shulamite needs to know the Shepherd-King better. She has known Him in part. She has known Him as lover; now she must enlarge her vision. Now she needs to know His station.

Because the daughters of Jerusalem are in charge of scene shifts, it is their words being spoken. Their words cry out: "Who is This?" The Shulamite has known the King <u>without</u> a vision of His power and magnitude. She has felt His arms, heard His words, received His invitations, and introduced Him to her family without knowing the force of His station. She has been taught His tenderness and experienced His patience; now it is time to behold His power.

Disciples who had been a long time with Jesus were questioned similarly; they were asked: "Whom say ye that I am?" They had known Him as a close associate and tender friend, but it was time for them to know His station. Their reply, He was the Son of the Living God, was met with a heavenly tribute for such revelation originated with the Father. There are church members by the thousands who have not come to this place in their walk with God. Yet every person in the kingdom must see Him in power before they can walk in His power. This scene carries a powerful impact on the life of the Shulamite.

Center stage is filled with splendor. Coming forth out of columns of smoke is the Son of God. As Solomon is the son of the King, so Jesus is the Son of THE KING. Solomon knew what an inheritor of power acted like; he portrays Jesus, who is the inheritor of His Father God, revealing His power. There are columns of smoke and much splendor painted into this scene because that was the way it was when the Lord of glory entered the temple. When Solomon dedicated the Temple, smoke filled it. Smoke filling the Temple of Solomon's day indicated the Presence of God. Out of the pillars of smoke (the Presence of the Almighty) steps Jesus! Behold Him, O Shulamite! (Bride) Here comes the Son of God, magnificent in fresh anointing (myrrh) and perfumed by incense reserved for the worship of God.

Powders of spices adorn the Son. (Spices of merchants were reserved only for Kings. Too expensive for the ordinary citizen, only Kings could afford to adorn themselves with such perfume. Exotic spices from around the world were common in Solomon's court.) He is King! O Shulamite, it is the King. He is the one who has held you and loved you. You thought you knew Him, but He is more than you imagined. Such is the manner of the anointing! After hearing him preach for the first time, a woman engaged to Charles G. Finney, the evangelist, asked him not to touch her for a moment. Finney was puzzled by her request and asked why? She explained, "Charles, I have known you as Charles, my lover and husband to be, but tonight when you preached, I saw you as an angel of light with a shining sword and I was frightened." (The Shulamite would have understood the future Mrs. Finney's emotion.) Isaiah 6 reveals the experience of the prophet when He saw the "King high and lifted up." Every believer must come to terms with the awesomeness of his or her Lover. His kingdom is without end; His power without equal.

"BEHOLD HIS BED,..." (SONG 3:7,KJV)

The daughters point to the King's bed. Clearly this is a palanquin, the kind of bed ridden or used by ancient kings. The bottom is of gold. The rods used for lifting are of silver. Like the ark of long ago, it is carried on the shoulders of men. The message of truth also has been carried on the shoulders of men throughout centuries. Born as a light burden on the shoulders of those made holy by the fiat of God, the duties to the ark were given to priests. The cargo of the ark was a reminder of the power of the Word. The Ten Commandments, Aaron's rod, and the pot of manna stood as testimony to the Old Covenant. The Old Testament shows the threefold testimony of God resting on the shoulders of men. Their duty was to carry this testimony with them wherever they went. The New Testament has no less a responsibility and privilege.

Truth accompanies power (and provision) as proof God keeps His Word. Now we see another ark, a palanquin, with One sitting on the place designed for the mercy seat. His blood, which represents Him, sits there in the eternal temple today as living testimony to the Covenant. Riding above the Law is the embodiment of a new law: the Law of Love. His New Covenant is exalted above the old Covenant. When we look on Him we see Truth; we see Power; we see Provision. He is all the Old plus the New. He is the fulfillment of all the Law. His grace supersedes all other considerations. (The book of Hebrews is wholly given to proving this mighty point.)

Jesus is now shown as the triumphant One, having done all that is necessary to redeem mankind. He rests in peace, having fulfilled every aspect of the Law. The Old covenant, based on animal blood, is superceded by His own blood. Zechariah prophesied He would ride on "a colt the foal of an ass" (Zech.9:9). He did. (This prophecy was fulfilled in His historic entry into Jerusalem fitted with palm branches and heralded by its citizens. There, His lowly estate befitted His sacrifice yet to come. Now, He rides in splendor for His sacrifice is complete.) Zechariah did not stop here. Prophets see in the distance. They often do not differentiate between near and far events. Sometimes they report both cases as simultaneous events. Zechariah sees two events. The near is Jesus entrance into Jerusalem where men accompanied Him with palm branches. The far is the entrance we see in the Song. (No need for chariot or horses and battle bow, for He has palanquin, shoulders, and warriors with the sword of the Spirit.)

Within the prophecy of Zechariah are all the elements found in Song 3:6-11. We see the people of Zion raised up and becoming like the "sword of a mighty man." The daughter of Zion and Jerusalem are both adjourned. The Lord coming forth from the wilderness is also similar. Even the new wine of Pentecost in Zechariah 9:15 is evidenced. But look at the crown spoken of in verse 16.

> "And the Lord their God shall save them in that day as the flock of his people: for they shall be as the stones of a crown, lifted up as an ensign upon His land." (KJV)

Look at the Song account considering all the prophet spoke. Review the power of the scene. The New Covenant is borne on the shoulders of warriors, not Priests consecrated by ritual Law. These are warriors proved in battle. They enter with the King and surround Him. They are strong in the Lord and the power of His might. To carry Him is their delight for He is not a burden but a privilege. "His burden is light and His yoke is easy!"

Attention is drawn to the silver and the gold of this bed, but greater attention is focused on the pavements of Love. (Some analysts attribute the embroidered seat to an act of love by the daughters of Jerusalem just for the King. Some see the seat of Love as a riding place for the daughters of Jerusalem. I see the seat of Love as a place of equality shared by the Bride. The Bride will share this bed and emblematically so will the daughters.)

Sixty mighty men of valor, accustomed to war, are at the King's side. Their swords are on their thighs. A state of readiness is about them. Protection of the highest rank is imposed on this scene, for He is surrounded by men of valor. Courageous men are these who have swords which well could have stood for the Word of God (sharp two-edged swords). These are men who were like Gideons' 300, although even a more elite group. These are experts in spiritual warfare. Experts in spiritual warfare are fewer than the masses. These are the valiant of True Israel.

Threescore in number, they signify a very small group in relation to the task. Could it be Solomon chose this exact number to coincide with sixty queens in Chapter 6:8? Examine the reason for their presence: FEAR. That which is the opposite of faith demands their skills. Fear, the opponent of the believer, still lurks in the darkness of the night. His dramatic entry is for the benefit of the Bride. This is not to be construed as Jesus second coming. This entry declares darkness still to be out there; therefore, defense is necessary. They know how to battle darkness.

Few are they who are expert in battling the darkness! Yes, there are thousands running about shouting this, or declaring that, or repeating catchy phrases, but they do not prevail against fear found in the night. As the Roman soldier was identified with His sword (for he was at one with His armament), so are these warriors. The sword of Spirit and Word is ready at their side. They number 60.

Those who work in biblical numerology will immediately jump to their texts for help in the number 60, and they will find nothing. Some facts are not gleaned so handily. I, too, sought commentators and texts for assistance in discovering why Solomon placed such emphasis on the number of warriors and queens; I have found nothing. (With faith I went into prayer seeking the Lord as to the significance of this passage. Because the Lord placed emphasis on this number, I had to seek <u>His</u> understanding. After three weeks of intermittent prayer and constant travail, I simply said, "Lord, I know you will reveal this passage, and I rest the matter in your hands."

In Taos, New Mexico, I awakened one morning with a startlingly clear understanding of the number 60. Israel was composed of twelve tribes. From Judah, Jesus came as King. Therefore, Judah was represented by Jesus (Solomon). Remove the tribe of Judah from the twelve tribes and there are eleven. Among the remaining eleven tribes there was Levi, the priestly tribe. They were allotted no land for inheritance. Levi was represented in the Shulamite (Believer-Bride) who was made a "king-priest" unto Her God. A reigning priest (King-Priest) was unheard of in the Old Covenant but not the New. In the Shulamite, we find the reigning priest. Just as Jesus is a Reigning Priest, so His Bride shares His station. His invitation to her is to share the seat of Love with Him. So, we remove the priestly tribe of Levi as Levi is represented by the Bride. The remaining tribes of true Israel would then number 10. Genesis 42 shows Israel was 10 in number once before. Israel needed a saviour because of their famine, and Joseph was that saviour. The story goes that his brethren, although strong, could not be more than burden bearers, for they were desolate without their saviour. When coupled with more truth, a similar picture is formed with the warriors in the Song. The number of man is 6. All the days of earth's years are six. The mystery is about to unfold. Ten multiplied by 6 equals the number of warriors herein described. Israel has borne the King on their shoulders for all the days of mankind. They were the ones who battled giants and territories filled with demons; true Israel still wages spiritual warfare and is accustomed to battle and the wage of fierce combat. (They may be portrayed as Queens in Chapter 6, but here, in Chapter 3, they are warriors who gladly bear their King.)

Get this picture: King Jesus, the Word, is riding on the willing shoulders of men, bearing Truth to the world of darkness, with trained spiritual warriors going forth unafraid to battle the night. Two beds are now contrasted: the bed of the Shulamite and the bed of the King. The Shulamite is content with her bed of comfort, but His bed is one of comfort *and* splendor. She overtly chooses His bed as opposed to remaining in her own. When she steps into the night to search for Him and finds Him, she takes Him to her family bedside and, after the columns of smoke scene, chooses His bed to be her own. (What the "non-bride church" is comfortable and satisfied with is nothing in comparison to what is offered the true Bride.) He, who had no place to lay His head on the earth, knew what He had abandoned to redeem His Bride. He has now a splendrous bed. See Him now crowned with the jeweled crown of Zechariah. See Him crowned by mother Israel (Rev. 12) ready for His bride!

To comprehend the depth of this scene, it is necessary to view it in the perspective given. The King wants the Shulamite to know Him in full spectrum. He allows her to see beyond the immediate, the intimate, the joyous togetherness they share. Just as the Banquet Hall broke into her "shepherd girl" mentality, this scene breaks into her limited view. This scene gives vent to the action which is to follow, but like the Banquet Hall, it will take her time to absorb its impact. Up to now, His ardor has been guarded and His words few. Now the dam is broken, and His great love for His intended creates a river of praise. If there was any doubt in Her mind as to Her place with Him, it must surely vanish in the presence of His love. He pours Himself out to her, for it is His nature. As He poured out His life before the Father for her redemption, He holds nothing back from Her now.

"BEHOLD THOU ART FAIR MY LOVE;..."(SONG 4:1, KJV)

Do not mistake Jesus' words for a lover's banter! They are calculated and full of meaning. Imagine the Lord, with His command of language, using the full range of His capability to make love to His intended. From a glad heart, He speaks freely to His Bride. She is not hindered in her hearing by religions' clamor. She relishes his libation. Her ears hear!

CHAPTER SEVEN

GOING TO THE GARDEN

"A garden enclosed is my sister, my spouse;" (Song 4:12a,KJV)

"...THOU ART FAIR, MY LOVE;...(Song 4:1,KJV)"

Chapter 4 of the Song ends with a garden scene which is so significant, I chose a passage toward the end of the fourth chapter as the title of chapter seven. Running through Song 4 are two themes; both of which are directed toward the Shulamite. The first theme is the "magnificence of her beauty." It is an overwhelming display of her personal beauty which gathers its color from the Old Testament. I call this first theme: "the New You."

Solomon challenges the Shulamite to view herself through His eyes and take into account her new position in Him. Like self-fulfilling prophecy, He projects her new image in terms of what she will become, not what she presently manifests. The act of her "becoming the Bride" is conditioned on her continued union with Him. She is in the process of becoming what is already evident before Him. He, again, is calling that which is not as though it actually was. She is in the process of being that wife spoken of in Ephesians 5:27:

> "That he might present it to himself a glorious church, not having spot, or wrinkle, or ANY SUCH THING; but that it should be **holy** and **without blemish**." (KJV)

The second theme of this chapter is not dissimilar to the first. Whereas the first theme is a didactic revelation of what is transpiring within her spiritual character, the second reveals the cause of the transformation. Hence, the second theme I call: "the Garden of the Heart."

Remind yourself Solomon had an intellect which superseded that of any man on earth. I Kings 4:29-31 (Amplified Version) says:

"And God gave Solomon exceptionally much wisdom and understanding, and breadth of mind like the sand of the seashore. Solomon's wisdom excelled the wisdom of all the people of the east, and all the wisdom of Egypt. For he was wiser than all other men;..."

In a later verse, the scripture declares Solomon wrote 1005 Songs, but this Song is openly declared in superlative terms as the "Song of Songs." Its superlative character rises to a pinnacle in the penning of this chapter. He makes reference casually to locations and objects which, if examined, are not casual. They are fully intended to build images within the Shulamite which will stand out in her memory. Attached to his words are pictures to be grasped and examined as one might examine a fine diamond or prism while searching for new hues of light and hidden beauty. These are not words tossed out without careful intent.

These are not the kind of words spoken hurriedly to a lover in anticipation of acceptance, with eyes searching her face for approval. These words are not transitory in order to be changed if they meet with wonder or dismay. Their intent is to position themselves in her heart in such a way as to be a monument, a foundation against any current of thought which might seek to enter and destroy her. These are the King's descriptions, His appropriations, His evaluations. All other considerations fall down before His words, for He speaks only the truth.

When the King says the Shulamite is "fair," she is fair! He drives home this fact with a repetitious statement as He has done in previous passages. "Thou art fair," is not a reiteration of previous declarations; it is spoken as if these words were used for the first time. This is a new and fresh appraisal which comes AFTER her experience with the watchmen. Through His eyes, she sees herself. It is as if He is looking at her afresh. In wonderment He might be paraphrased into adding: "you really are fair; you really are."

One might imagine the King holding His love while speaking these words. His imagery is not peripheral (in general terms) as in other passages, for He is speaking in most specific terms. Readers know from His descriptions

He is more than slightly acquainted with the Shulamite. He addresses her with an intimate knowledge of her person. Whether His intent is to reveal just how intimately He does know her, or simply to state the facts of His fore-knowledge is not told. From this relationship will never come words like, "Depart from me, I never knew you."

Intimate knowledge is the hallmark of the bond between these lovers. Their love is defined in the "no secrets" nature of their interaction. (Formal churches can never approach this type of interaction; it is not within their framework.) Like death, once this type of intimacy is entered into, there is no retreat. Soon, the death comparison will appear (8:6), and you will see this fact expressed. The Bride's responses toward the end of this chapter are ignited by the King's passion now. She is overwhelmed by what she experiences in His observations.

"COME WITH ME..." (SONG 4:8, KJV)

Sandwiched in between the two themes is the constant invitation for the Shulamite to join the King in a more intimate involvement (4:8). Never lose sight of His desire for her to "come away" with Him. It is better to be hand in hand while learning the ways of Jesus than trying to learn of Him "from afar." "From afar" is no longer acceptable for these last days. God is finished with "from afar." Both of them have experienced all the "from afar" they are willing to tolerate. Since Moses, the "from afar" motif has always ended in sorrow and error. This "come away" will end in love, power, sound mind, and the intimacy of a marriage.

"...THOU HAST DOVE'S EYES..." (SONG 4:1, KJV)

Looking into the eye of another person is an informative endeavor. Investigators, physicians, and counselors often utilize this method to determine the inner being of a person. Having a "single" eye precludes the hypocrite who has learned to "look one straight in the eye and lie like a dog." As in other places in this Song, the bride is applauded for having "dove's eyes." Since Solomon uses this phrase over and over in his appraisal of her beauty, there needs to be one further emphasis gleaned from it. The "single eye" is the sole ingredient used to produce the "fair" attribute which is synonymous with "holiness." The dove of the Spirit has not only come upon her but also dwells within her. His qualities are evident in her speech, choices, and life style. He has image-changing capabilities that transform damaged souls to those without wrinkle or spot. His greatest joy is to see sin erode under His gentle hand. In words as tender as a lover, the Spirit speaks to the Bride about things which are unpleasing and unacceptable to the Bridegroom. Her response is "help me take those things from me." (When the quality decision to be the Bride of Jesus enters the believer's heart, all other considerations are of no importance.)

The Bride listens to the Spirit, does what the Spirit directs her to do, and welcomes His voice. If He prompts her to stop, she stops. If He whispers to go, to stand, to listen, to wait, to speak this, or be silent on that, all this is within the scope of His authority. Those in the faith hall of fame, cited in Hebrews 11, are the ones whose lives followed the Spirit's rule. They had "dove's eyes."

"...THY HAIR..." (SONG 4:1, KJV)

Next, the Bridegroom turns to "a woman's glory," her hair.

> "Thy hair is as a flock of goats, that appear from mount Gilead." (Song 4:1 KJV)

Doubtless, if a modern lover used such a phrase, he might meet with total bewilderment. Be careful to note the reference is modified by the use of Gilead. If emphasis is placed on the color or texture of goats in general, then black, or amber, or some other goat color is all that is meant. Location, not hair color, is the most significant factor in this verse. Gilead must be the focal point for our inquiry. Gilead is a reference that takes study to understand why it is chosen for this specific moment.

Solomon's wisdom prescribes Gilead to be the specific region or place of consideration for a purpose. Run some references on Gilead, and numerous events come to the forefront. Here, the sons of Joseph were given the land of Gilead as their inheritance. The men who bought Joseph from his brothers (at the insistence of Judah) came from Gilead. The Lord must have had a sense of humor in giving the land of those who captured Joseph to be Joseph's inheritance. The Lord was creating a sort of "one-upmanship" for him. The Lord vindicates His own!

At Gilead, Jephthah resided and caused a yearly event among the daughters of Zion to take place. They mourned his daughter's loss. For Gilead, King Ahab lost his life, and the false prophets loathed it.

Ramoth in Gilead was opened as a city of refuge among ten other cities so designed. Lying east of the Jordan and north of Judah, there are many references which include Gilead as a boundary.

David discovered "mighty men" came from Gilead. Perhaps the "mighty men of valour" in the previous chapter originated in Gilead. Although Gilead was occupied with men of valour, it fell before the hand of the Lord. Thus, it becomes a location which illustrates that no area of fortification can escape the power and might of our God. In Deuteronomy 2:36, we learn:

> "From Aroer, which is on the edge of the Arnon valley, and from the city that is in the valley, as far as Gilead, there was no city too high and strong for us; the Lord our God delivered all to us."
> (Amplified Version)

Gilead stands as a reminder of the power of the Lord to carry out His will through men of covenant. Gilead represents man working with the Lord by faith. But the vibrant meaning of Gilead, as it pertains to the Song, comes from the lips of Jeremiah. He writes about a time in the future when the people of God will have ultimate victory.

> "And I will bring Israel (home) again to his fold and pasturage, and he shall feed (on the most fertile districts both west and east) on Carmel and Bashan, and <u>his soul shall be satisfied upon the hills of Ephraism and in Gilead.</u> In those days and at that time, says the Lord, the iniquity of Israel shall be sought for, and there will be none; and the sins of Judah, and none shall be found; for I will pardon those whom I cause to remain as a remnant (the reserved ones, who come forth after the long tribulation).
> (Jeremiah 50:19-20 Amplified Version)

From Gilead, Moses viewed the promised land. In Gilead, Jacob built an altar and made a Covenant. Its balm is the desire of those who want to be healed, and in its heights of 2000 feet, forests and rich pastures (abundance) abound. Solomon carefully chose Gilead for his analogy because he saw it as a place of promise as did Jeremiah. (Remember, eyes focused entirely on Jesus and set between victorious parameters {her hair} are what this verse is really about.)

"THY TEETH..." (SONG 4:2, KJV)

The Bride's face is still before the King as His compliments continue. By now it is plain Solomon does not make reference lightly. The King's attention turns to the region of the mouth. Emphasis is not on a healthy arrangement of teeth. That they are even, with no gaps and beautifully cared for, is not the sum of meaning. True, the smile of a beautiful woman is enhanced by such an arrangement as described but, knowing Solomon, meaning lies beyond. Carefully, He focuses on the mouth of His Bride. Words like "washing," "twins," "scarlet thread," and "pomegranates" are not haphazardly chosen. His use of "flock" instead of focusing on one sheep is significant. Abundance characterizes those things relative to the Bride. "Twins" is used two ways: first as abundance, second to signify "similarity, or likeness." He quickly sums up His compliment with "thy speech is comely." Here is the key. From the region of the mouth come declarations of Faith or the profanity of denial. Simon Peter characterizes this truth in his words to the three inquirers during the trial of Jesus.

The speech of the saints is "Jesus talk." Matthew 26:73 (KJV) says:

> "And after a while came unto him they that stood by, and said to Peter, Surely thou also art one of them; for thy SPEECH bewrayeth thee."

Simon's reply is a worldly curse to distinguish between the holy and the profane. He shows the difference between the clean and the unclean. His lips speak differently than his inner man. Bitter and sweet water does not come from the same well. By words, every idle one, every man will be judged; Simon judged himself and wept.

Allow me, for clarity's sake, to use a paraphrase of Solomon's descriptions: "The Bride's lips, in similarity and likeness to his (like twins), speak words "washed" by His blood (the scarlet thread) and her speech is not "barren (but fruitful)."

The "barren" bear no children, even the very word "barren" cursed the soul of Rachel. Isaiah 54 declares that the days of barrenness are gone. The bride is not barren! The Bride's words are fruit filled. Words of life and faith issue from her lips, words which are "comely" in the King's eyes come out of her. (In later verses, she will pour forth praises to Him from her anointed mouth.)

"...A THREAD OF SCARLET,..." (SONG 4:3,KJV)

As we look into the meaning of the scarlet thread, it will be necessary to incorporate other descriptors used in verse 2. For instance, in verse two, we did not elaborate on the word washing. Now it is necessary to include this word, for it relates to our study of the scarlet thread.

Ceremonial washing, as well as the use of a scarlet thread dipped in the blood of a red heifer, has powerful significance here. Hebrews 9:19 says:

> "For when every command of the Law had been read out by Moses to all the people, he took the blood of slain calves and goats, together with water and scarlet wool, and with a bunch of hyssop sprinkled both the Book (the roll of the Law and covenant) itself, and all the people. Saying these words: This is the blood that seals and ratifies the agreement (the testament, the covenant) which God commanded (me to deliver to) you."
>
> (Amplified Version)

Every place where the Hebrew word *shani* (scarlet) has been used as it is used in the Song, has reference in some manner to holy use. Holy use is use in worship or ceremony. Only two references are outside these boundaries. Genesis 38 pictures a scarlet thread in the birth of the last born children of Judah. They were twins.

One of the twins threw forth his hand, and the midwife bound it with a scarlet thread and declared he was the first born. That twin brought his hand back into the womb, and his brother was born first. If we perceive the grave as a womb, then we understand that Jesus was the first born from the grave. The first born from the grave did not have the "scarlet thread," but those of us who come after Him will be characterized by it. As surely as the "first born from the grave" was resurrected, so will we who have been cleansed by His blood.

The other use of the word *shani*, outside ceremonial reference, is found in II Samuel 1:24. David instructs the daughters of Israel to weep upon Saul's death. He declares that Saul "clothed you in scarlet and other delights." Again, the reference is not without parallel to the provision of Jesus for His Bride. He has clothed His bride in His blood bought redemption, and at His right are "pleasures" for evermore (Ps.16:11)."

The Genesis and Samuel passages, when taken together with Jesus' emphasis on speech, causes certain conclusions to be drawn. One conclusion is that the speech of the Bride is the "washed by the blood" kind of speech. Another is that speaking through scarlet lips causes "Bride-speech." "Bride-speech" is from the same source as "Jesus talk." Her speech reflects the purity and holiness of her relationship with Jesus. What comes from her mouth is like what you will hear from His. A reference to scarlet lips is more than a casual comment!

"...THY SPEECH IS COMELY:..." (SONG 4:3 KJV)

Vital to faith is the link between speech and faith. Nearly every act of belief begins with a confession. Whether it is an act of believing for mountains to be moved or the first confession of a repentant sinner in response to Romans, speaking is the key. To be like Jesus, who spoke only what He heard from the Father, is the pattern for every believer.

It is imperative to speak our words as Jesus spoke His. After conversation with the Father and through the leadership of the Spirit, Jesus spoke the Father's will into the earth. The Holy Spirit himself often lays on the believer's heart what the Father and the Son wish to be spoken into the earth. Jesus' spoken words became the written word of the Bible. Our spoken words join with His, and we become His living agents on the earth. His agency is the spoken word of the saints. When we openly speak His words into the earth, our speech changes the earth.

In prayer, we are led in what to pray. In witness, we are prompted by the Spirit in terms we could never have reckoned. Whether in the privacy of our homes or in circumstances involving the world beyond our homes, we are to be aware of our words. Words build or break, and they become examples of James' teaching. James taught the tongue starts fires. Those fires can burn temples or start revivals. Through our words, we are known. Through our words, our inner man is expressed; through our words, our values are exchanged. What is important enough to talk about must be to us important! (Oh, that our Lover would hear us praise Him, speak our inner most thoughts to Him, share with Him—then would we be judged "comely." Oh, that He would hear us speaking His words to the world, calling into existence that which is not, but must be: "through comely speech.")

"...THY TEMPLES ARE LIKE A PIECE OF POMEGRANATE..." (SONG 4:3, KJV)

Her lover continues to praise her by using a reference to "pomegranates" which most interpreters believe is an erotic reference. At best, they attribute its presence to a symbol of fertility. Partly, they are correct. If, however, you continue with a holy theme, greater significance might point to the use of the pomegranate as it relates to the skirt of the high priest.

At the bottom of the high priest's robe were pomegranates interspersed with bells. With every step, the ringing of the bells and the presence of the symbol for "abundance in life" utilize vision and sound to portray a "declaration of life." Life and abundance characterize the intent of Jesus for His Bride.

Here, the pomegranate is used to show fertility of mind. The Bride's temples are singled out. *Raqqah*, the Hebrew word for this part of the head (or upper cheek region) refers to the seat of intelligence. We might put these symbols together with this comment: "Lips that speak precious words are not connected to a stultified minds." Solomon uses the pomegranate theme for her temples to show fertility of mind, a mind where good seed is planted and a harvest is sure. In the mind of the true Bride is held the true history of the church. (Hers is not a seminarian view of church history. In her mind is mulled the intercession of saints who have never reached sainthoods' recognition. In her mind the languish of prisons, the cry of the tortured, and the endless flow of tears are all present. Hers is a different intelligence than that of the world, for she incorporates Hebrews 11:33-40.)

Enfolded in the Bride's mind is a rich history of valiant souls of faith. Her thoughts are on what is pure, lovely, and of good report. She is the true Bride, with a mental state which matches the Kings. Here, the Holy Spirit finds a welcome depository for "things that are to come." Here, the words of Jesus are readily brought to mind. Here, spiritual wisdom is manifested. Here, wonderful ideas are formulated to enhance the ministry, finance the cause of the kingdom, and carry out the command to "go to the nations." She is the faithful servant with the ten talents. She is the prepared virgin with lamps trimmed and oil at hand. She is the virtuous woman. She has the mind of Christ.

"THY NECK IS LIKE THE TOWER OF DAVID..."
(SONG 4:4, KJV)

Behold her beauty! How lovely is her neck which is not bowed in shame or defeat. It is a neck "like the tower of David" which was built for a fortress and a repository for weapons of battle. This is not the neck of a depressed, deranged, and downtrodden wreck. She is so described to reveal the inner power she possesses. Straight and erect she stands for a world to admire her beauty. Attack her, and see how quickly her mind works in co-ordination with her inner love.

"...whereon there hang a thousand bucklers, all shields of mighty men." (Song 4:4 KJV)

A thousand shields of faith depict a state of preparedness. The true Bride is not a weak child unprepared for battle. Hear her tongue speak faithfilled promises. Hear her Words pronounce victory before the battle! With eyes on her task and the mental acumen equal to the situation, she rises to her heights and meets every challenge.

(Oh, might the church get a glimpse of who the Bride really is. Oh, that a world could hear only the true Bride speak, and view her in action. How different would be their view. The gates of Hell tremble at such a thought!)

"THY TWO BREASTS ARE LIKE... TWINS,..."
(SONG 4:5, KJV)

Yet, in all of her power, the Bride is still the woman. Let us not lose the fact she is the Second Eve. Her breasts are the place of nurture where the "sincere milk of the Word" is obtained. She cuddles her new born and helps them grow. This true church, with no plan but Jesus plan, no agenda but His agenda, fulfills her role as nurturer with the same perfection as she meets her challengers. A perfection relegated and a perfection earned is this marvel of the ages, the Bride. He finds her "all fair, my love; there is no spot in thee."

In just a few more verses, we will find the cost of such perfection. We will note the "quality decision" the Bride made which gave her these attributes. This is not some diatribe of meaningless phrases. This is no Sunday morning service filled with sweet pieties. What we will soon view is the inner heart of one who has determined anything which was displeasing to Jesus must be weeded out. She is the one who pulled up every disparaging plant in her heart and rendered Jesus to be Lord of her life. Her decision costs many "precious" things but none more precious than Him. What she is hearing from Him now made time and preciseness worth it all. Toiling in prayer and being attentive to every urging of the Spirit, she has become the beautiful Bride He desires. She has worked out her own salvation with fear and trembling and is now beside Him. There are no words of deprecation about her "sad estate" as first we heard in the opening verses. She has ascertained her role through interaction with Him. She stands beside Him, a figure of beauty who will yet grow more beautiful until there shall be none to compare with her in all the universe.

"UNTIL THE DAY BREAK, AND THE SHADOWS FLEE AWAY,... (SONG 4:6,KJV)"

Peculiarly enough, Solomon interjects basically the same words of Song 2:17 again in Song 4:6. The passage in 2:17 is an appeal by the Bride to: "give me time to comprehend all that has been displayed before me (paraphrased)." This second passage (4:6) is spoken by the Bridegroom and reflects His understanding of her need for reflection.

The Bridegroom is leaving in order for the Bride to be alone, but not for very long. This is a different set of circumstances than we found in the banquet hall. Just after the banquet scene, while still immature, the Bride defines her terms. Now, the Bridegroom prescribes for her a brief repose which is based on mutual terms. He knows her, and she knows Him on a deeper level. His declaration then is not just His will over hers but the outcropping of their mutual wills. He has just demonstrated great intuitiveness. He has just clothed her in verbal garments. Lest she be overwhelmed with all she experiences, He declares He will return to the Mountain of His Fathers' Presence.

"The mountain of myrrh and the hill of frankincense" is where Jesus dwells at this very moment in history. He is the High Priest of our prayers and, by the Holy Spirit, is in constant intercession for us. He wants us to gain intuitiveness (word of wisdom, word of knowledge). He is giving His Bride time to grow in grace and spiritual knowledge. He expects this growth to be progressive and does not expect it to take forever!

Two words in the King's declaration should bear scrutiny, for they are peculiar to the Song. These words are "break" and "shadows." The Hebrew word *puach* means "to break or breathe." This word is only used in the Song passages and no where else in any scriptural text. Isn't that fact enough to make it worth looking into? I believe *pauch* has to do with a breakthrough in thinking similar to a student who breathes a sigh of relief and exclaims, "I finally see it; it has really dawned on me; I see what is being said!"

Another word which is only used in the Song and in a reference to Jeremiah 6:4ff (The whole prophetic utterance in the sequence is about the shadows of the evening.) is the Hebrew word *tsel.* Most commonly, *tsel* refers to a shadow like the shadow of a tree or the shadow of a mountain. However, the plural form of the word is unique to the Song and to a passage in Jeremiah. Because these are the only two places the plural form is used in scripture, it would lead one to believe there is a link. In the Song, "shadows" signify the lingering remains of night and darkness. These "shadows" are dispelled by the coming dawn.

In the Jeremiah passage, the "shadows" are gathering. The day is ending and time is running out. Jeremiah is calling for the destruction of a vile woman who is known for her wickedness. Jeremiah 6:7:

> "As a fountain casteth out her waters, so she casteth our her wickedness: violence and spoil is heard in her; before me continually is grief and wounds." (KJV)

Both passages deal with a woman (no longer the "shepherd girl"). Both are beautiful and delicate. In the Song, the woman strives in her love and devotion to please her Lover. In Jeremiah, she is totally given to disgracing, disobeying, and insulting her Lover. In the Song, she is characterized in a later passage as being "a garden enclosed" with a living fountain within. In the Jeremiah passage, she is a fountain "continually casting out fresh wickedness (Amplified Version)." In the Song, the planting of the Lord is to be found in her heart. In the Jeremiah passage, "violence," "destruction," " sickness" and "wounds" are within her (Jer.6:7). In the Song, she is applauded for her righteousness and the beauty it has bestowed on her. In Jeremiah 6:16, she is instructed to "ask for the eternal paths, where is the good, old way; then walk in it (Amplified)."

Further in Jeremiah's prophecy, the Lord explains himself:

> "For in the day that I brought them out of the land of Egypt, I did not speak to your fathers or command them concerning burnt offerings or sacrifices. But this thing I did command them:

Listen to and obey My voice, and I will be your God, and you shall be My people; and walk in the whole way that I command you, that it may be well with you." (Jeremiah 7:23 Amplified)

Further in that same chapter is verse 34 where the consequences of not following His commands are laid out:

"Then will I cause to cease from the cities of Judah and from the streets of Jerusalem the voice of the bridegroom and the voice of the bride; for the land shall become a waste." (Amplified)

In the Song, the voice of the bride and the voice of the Bridegroom combine to make a mighty statement of unity. Notice in the Jeremiah passage the main judgment for not obeying the voice of the Lord is the absence of the bridegroom and the bride. The Song is the glorification of the Bridegroom, and the Bride and is evidence they have obeyed the voice of God. The Shulamite is learning not to "obey" so much as to "enter in."

Jeremiah finishes his treatise on the state of Israel by comparing it to dross and impure metals. As jewelers and artificers know, the sputtering sign of impurities being burned away is evidence of their mingled state with the pure gold. The fire tries them, and the assayer, who examines the remaining silver or gold, makes a decision as to the level of purity. He then stamps his approval by certifying it. The Bride's heart is pure. Her quality decision to "hear Him out" and seek to be as "one" with Him yielded a good appraisal from the "Chief assayer." She is pure gold, not the dross found in Jeremiah. Jesus is the assayer, not the prophet in Jeremiah 6:27. Gone are the days when any other appraisal but His is significant. Not the preachers, not the prophets, not the established religious order, only the opinion of Jesus is what counts. I don't know about you, but that is good news!

"COME WITH ME..." (SONG 4:8, KJV)

After the Bride's short period of assimilation of the truths she has learned, a fresh invitation is given. This invitation is similar to 2:13 and 7:11. The King invites her to learn first hand by walking and talking with Him. Entering into His life, rather than being separated by time, place, and commitment, calls her into a new dimension of unity. His invitation is constantly before her, whether she is willing to accept it is the only inhibition. He never demands she follow Him – He only invites. This is akin to the Holy Spirit who comes to us with invitations to stretch our faith, to walk with greater depth in our understanding, and to experience Him personally.

With the King's new invitation comes the Bride's new name, "My spouse." Again, He is prophetic as to her position in Him. She is not yet His spouse, but she will certainly attain that position and be complete in her faith when it happens. "My spouse" is a new commitment from Him to her. Listen! This is a two-way street. He is definitely in love with Her. He sees so much in her, so many qualities she has yet not seen in herself, His excitement builds. I firmly believe every day when Jesus looks down on His Bride, He turns to the Father and asks: "Is this the day?"

The King's invitation is rife with symbols. Some interpreters say the word "from" in Song 4:8, actually means "to." They perceive its meaning as an invitation to go to the heights of the mountains with Him. I do not share their view. While they emphasize the heights' concept, I emphasize the location. Looking into the mountain locations yields its own reward. I also find other meanings which are not tied to the mountains to be interesting. Lebanon, Amana, Shenir, and Hermon are specific locations, and they have import within themselves. They are not just handy mountain peaks used without other significance.

When Solomon says to "Come with me _from_ Lebanon, my spouse," He is inviting his Bride to join Him for a reason. It may mean to come away from the judgment that will be upon "Lebanon" as spoken of in Isaiah 10:33-34:

> "Behold, the Lord, the Lord of hosts, shall lop the bough with terror: and the high ones of stature shall be hewn down, and the haughty shall be humbled. And he shall cut down the thickets of the forest with iron, and Lebanon shall fall by a mighty one." (KJV)

Another reason may be that after the judgment of Lebanon, the prophecy of His coming can then be fulfilled.

He is inviting His Bride to leave the places of judgment to facilitate His coming again. It does matter where the Bride resides. If she lives in a place where judgment must take place before Jesus can be exalted, then she must leave that place. I firmly believe this is the meaning of "come ye out from among them" which is found in the New Testament. It matters where you live, with what body you fellowship and where you invest your interest and time. If you are in a city, town, or village where judgment must fall, get out. If you fellowship with a denomination or congregation where judgment must fall, leave. If your occupation is in an area where judgment must come, find another occupation or interest. It matters where the Bride resides.

Look at the verse which follows the judgment for haughtiness, in Isaiah 11:1

> "And there shall come forth a rod out of the stem of Jesse, and a Branch shall grow out of his roots: And the Spirit of the Lord shall rest upon Him..." (KJV)

(Continue reading the Isaiah passage and glean from its other truths. Not desiring to quote the entire chapter of Isaiah 11, read its comments on the references regarding lions and leopards.)

Her lover calls the Bride away from judgment to a Saviour who is able to answer every test and supply her with great joy. A study of lions and leopards, as they symbolize judgment, can begin in Hosea 13:7ff:

> "Therefore I will be unto them as a lion: as a leopard by the way will I observe them:" (KJV)

The Lord continues the analogy of judgment by including a bear and then ends with an invitation:

> "O Israel, thou hast destroyed thyself; but in me is thine help." (Hosea 13:9 KJV)

The Bride, who has found herself in the place of impending judgment, must abandon that place, and like Abraham, she is to seek a country whose builder and maker is God. Remaining in the place of judgment is vexation akin to Lot and can only expose the Bride to undeserved pain.

"...FROM THE TOP OF ARMANA,..."(SONG 4:8,KJV)

Amana[1], Shenir[2], and Hermon[3] are types and shadows of the sanctuary of the Lord but here they are further locations filled with judgment. Although Amana is only used in the Old Testament in the Song, it shares in the judgment picture. Those not of Israel referred to mount Hermon as Shenir, but the Jews called it Hermon. The emphasis is not to leave just one place of judgment (Lebanon[4]) but to leave all places of judgment. This is the judgment that begins in the house of the Lord. There you have it, a clear call to leave the haughtiness of man, the deception of man, and the judgments on man. Our invitation is to come away with Him. Our place is with Him, and no compromise is acceptable.

Those who come with him from Lebanon will participate in the promise of Isaiah 16:5

> "And in mercy shall the throne be established: and he shall sit upon it in truth in the tabernacle of David, judging, and seeking judgment, and hasting righteousness."

Judgment with mercy is available to those who will leave behind all that is tainted with the control of man and come away with Him. Judgment without mercy will fall among those who stay behind refusing to hearken to His voice. To those who will hear His voice, Psalm 85:8-13 is very clear:

> "I will hear what God the LORD will speak: for he will speak peace unto his people, and to his saints: but let them not turn again to folly. Surely his salvation *is* nigh them that fear him; that glory may dwell in our land. Mercy and truth are met

---

[1]Amana means fixed, sustained, permanent.
[2]Shenir means snow covered peak
[3]Hermon means sublime, sanctuary.
[4]Lebanon means white mountain.

together; righteousness and peace have kissed *each other*. Truth shall spring out of the earth; and righteousness shall look down from heaven. Yea, the LORD shall give *that which is* good; and our land shall yield her increase. Righteousness shall go before him; and shall set *us* in the way of his steps.   (KJV)

"THOU HAS RAVISHED MY HEART,..."(SONG 4:9,KJV)

King Jesus now enters into a new form of praise to His Bride. I say "a new form" for truly the intensity is turned up. Gushing forth from His inner man comes a form of worship which is delicate to handle at this stage of interpretation. A premise must be established at this juncture. From Song 4:7 to the end of the book, it is as if the reader walks through a door into a new dimension. From this point forward, the intensity level of both partners is heightened. I say both partners, for it is now no longer the bantering style of "He gives her a compliment; she gives Him a compliment" type of conversation. Not to suggest that all before this is trite but to say it has taken this long for her to meet Him at this level. Had He poured out this libation of love to her from the beginning, she might still be running. Keep in mind that there are two images of the Bride in the Song: the Bride developing and the Bride complete. Both images are earth images. This is not the Queen of heaven. She is not yet the Bride of the marriage feast yet to take place. She is going to get there, though. She will make it. She will be there on time. She is about to find out just how important she is in heaven's plan.

"Thou hast ravished my heart, my sister, my spouse;"   (Song 4:9a KJV)

More than likely you will have to adjust to this higher level of inter-action. For Jesus to be smitten with His bride is not in the average book on doctrine and theology. He is saying, "You go right to my heart when you look at me like you do." (This is the only reference in the Bible to *labab*. It is translated as "ravished.") Jesus needs His Bride in order for Him to be complete. Just as the first Adam lacked completeness, so the Second Adam needs His Bride for completeness. He wants her to be beside Him. He desires she relate to Him. He is in love with her.

"My sister and my spouse" refer to the two images of the Song. In the world of being born into the kingdom, she is His sister. In her role in history, she is the Bride.

"...THOU HAST RAVISHED MY HEART WITH ONE OF THINE EYES,..." (SONG 4:9,KJV)

The Bride reaches into the King's heart with one glance from her eyes filled with love for Him. More than the spoken words are such glimpses between lovers. Transmissions between lovers in love are often winged in a single glance. The eye speaks louder sometimes than the lips. The turning of one eye toward her lover encourages further comment.

"...WITH ONE CHAIN OF THY NECK." (SONG 4:9,KJV)

Add to the "eye" passage the double meaning of the "chain of thy neck," and a landslide of tribute is about to take place. Solomon pens his earliest Proverbs about wearing the advice of his mother and father as chains on his neck. These are chains of freedom, not slavery. Worn like ornaments about the neck, the Word of God is constantly displayed as a witness of the inner transformation of the wearer. The Bride is beautiful to the Bridegroom, for she gracefully wears the ornaments of righteousness.

"HOW FAIR IS THY LOVE, MY SISTER, MY SPOUSE!..." (SONG 4:10,KJV)

With emboldened heart, the King says, "How fair is thy love, my sister, my spouse!" Her dual role, while being one person, is similar to the dual capacity of the Son. He is Son and Bridegroom. Many churches emphasize His Sonship and His position as Brother. Calls are often made to enter boldly into the presence of "our covenant brother," but few calls are made "to enter the arena of the spouse."

"...HOW MUCH BETTER IS THY LOVE THAN WINE!..." (SONG 4:10, KJV)

The Bride's love is better than wine, and her presence fragrances the King's life. She means more to Him than all other precious things. He drinks from her. She is better than fine wine. Within her flows love which, when tasted, offers greater reward than fine wine. Her lips speak anointed words. Her lips speak words that identify their source, the wine of the Living Word.

"...HONEY AND MILK ARE UNDER THY TONGUE;...
(SONG 4:11, KJV)

Ezekiel 3:3, shows the prophet eating the Word of the Lord given to Him and declaring it was sweet as honey to his mouth. Proverbs 24:13-14 (KJV) says:

> "My son, eat thou honey, because it is good; and the honeycomb, which is sweet to thy taste: So shall the knowledge of wisdom be unto thy soul: when thou hast found it, then there shall be a reward, and thy expectation shall not be cut off."

The Bride has evidence of having eaten the Word. Its presence is under her tongue. Supporting her speech is the power of the Word. When her tongue speaks, it is not wagging in gossip. When her tongue speaks, the Word comes forth. Words of wisdom and knowledge flow from her lips. Prayer based on the Word flows from her mouth. Her tongue has Canaan language in its speech. It is a place of milk and honey. When her tongue speaks, He listens!

Promised in Corinthians, the word of wisdom is evident on the Bride's tongue because she has eaten of the source. What is missing in the church of today is certainly not the word of knowledge. What is missing is the word of wisdom. What is found on her lips that is so pleasing to Jesus? The word of wisdom. That which is prophesied of Jesus is also found in her! Isaiah 7:15 (KJV) declares: "Butter (a milk produce) and honey shall He eat." Now, the Bride comes close to Him, and he sees she has tasted what He has tasted. That which caused Him to choose the good and reject the evil, abides in her! His land, flowing with milk and honey, is found in her. His Bride has the source of plenty working within her being; why, even her garments smell like His.

The smell of cedar, whom no insect dare penetrate, is on her. She is impenetrable by the influences of a world which might seek to destroy her. Lebanon (meaning white mountain) is not modified by lions and leopards now, but stands for impenetrable stateliness.

"A GARDEN ENCLOSED..." (SONG 4:12, KJV)

I call this section, the "garden of the heart." Within the heart of the Bride is the planting of the Lord. That is why she speaks with wisdom, and her person exudes fragrances pleasant to Him. From Song 4:12 to 5:1, we are ushered into one of the most beautiful and meaningful passages in this book. The garden of the heart is central to Jesus' teaching about the sower and the seed. Her heart is good ground. It is in her heart the Word flourishes and is not choked out or dried up. Satan cannot take away the sown Word in her heart, for it has a dedication on its gate: "His Garden."

"THY PLANTS ARE AN ORCHARD..." (SONG 4:13, KJV)

Although Solomon catalogues more fragrances and plants in the Song than is recorded in any other book of the Bible, our attention is not drawn to them. Our attention is the heart of the Bride in which is planted all the things from their being together. The walks, the talks, the attendant discussions about life and death, and the fruits of righteousness are all planted here. This is the same manner of planting David used with Solomon. This is the way of the believer and Jesus. Being together in the experiences of life, talking around the dinner table, talking while working with one another is how spiritual plants are planted in the heart garden.

The Hebrews were instructed to talk to their children, to experience certain feasts and observe rituals together for the same purpose. The heart garden is the place where the weeds of the world can be excised. True, Jesus taught at the end of the world He would separate the tares from the wheat, but while we are in this world, it is our duty to weed the garden of our own hearts.

"A garden enclosed is my sister, my spouse" opens the scene for our inspection. Around the Bride's heart is built a wall. A walled garden, whether walled by the King's love and protection or a garden walled by her own determination, makes little difference to the context. The protection of the contents in the garden is what is important. The precious seed of the Word must be protected until it grows in the heart. This is what is important. Protection means harboring the Word, cultivating it, watering it, working with it until blooms burst and fragrance the inner man.

"...A SPRING SHUT UP, A FOUNTAIN SEALED." (SONG 4:12,KJV)

Until now, the Bride has just had the <u>potential</u> for a heart garden, for without water, there could be no planting. With the water sealed away, there would have been no chance for the seed to grow. The fountain within her must be unsealed. The unsealing of the fountain of life within her comes as she perseveres in her quality decision about Jesus. Up until this, she has been the recipient of multiple plantings of truth and life. You can see it evidenced in her life.

Jesus spoke on the feast day saying:

> "If any man thirst, let him come unto me and drink, He that believeth on me, as the scripture hath said, out of his belly shall flow rivers of living water." (John 7:37-38 KJV)

The Spirit of God enters and sets the water flowing. Look into Revelation 22:17, and tell me who is talking:

> "And the Spirit **and** the bride say, Come. And let him that heareth say, Come. And let him that is athirst say Come. And whosoever will, let him take the water of life freely." (KJV)

By verse 15 of Song 4, the water is flowing. Streams of water pouring out of the Bride's garden, like the streams of Lebanon, water the Word. A well of living water is found in her like the one found in Ezekiel 47, where a stream of living water comes from the throne of God. Ezekiel swam over his head in those waters, finally to discover everywhere the water touched two things happened: Dead things came to life, and planted things flourished. The Bride of Jesus is full of this living water. The Living Water flows into the streets of cities, towns, and villages and all who encounter it are changed. It abounds to the misery of disease and death and overcomes them. It touches the untouchables and makes them whole. It flows from the heart of the Bride and Bridegroom to water the "planting of the Lord."

"...AN ORCHARD OF POMEGRANATES,..."
(SONG 4:13, KJV)

The orchard of pomegranates blooms where no fertility previously has existed. Because of the living water, babies are born. The orchard of pomegranates is a witness to the fertility of the soil and testifies to the bearing of much fruit. Pleasant fruits of the Spirit issue out from trees bowed down with their plenty. Healing comes to the nations from the camphor and the spikenard. The ingredients of "true worship" incense are grown here. The ingredients of the pure oil of the anointing are here.

In the garden of the heart, Jesus is welcome to walk. When He spoke to the woman at the well and said the time would come when men would not worship in Jerusalem or the mountain, He was talking about His garden. True worship takes place in the garden of the heart!

He who travailed in the garden of Gethsemane now walks in another garden which made Gethsemane worth it all. It is His delight to stride among His plantings and hear His bride say in low tones, "My darling, if you see anything in here that is not pleasing to you, tell me and I will remove it quickly." This is the reason for a "heart garden" scene. No bride can be without one.

To own the Word of God deep within the soil of your being, and to have it watered by the well of living water is something different from what most church members possess. Such does not come from casual reading of the Bible and short Sunday School tidbits. This is why the oil cannot be bought at the last minute, and fruit is not born of man's design.

"AWAKE, O NORTH WIND;...(SONG 4:16, KJV)"

Hear her heart cry:

"Awake, O north wind; and come thou South; blow upon the garden, that the spices thereof may flow out. Let my beloved come into his garden, and eat his pleasant fruits." (Song 4:16 KJV)

The Bride is aware who is the owner of the garden. Long ago, she abdicated her throne for the King's enthronement. Like a dramatist on the stage of life, she hurls a command to the cold, harsh, freezing North winds. "Come and blow on my garden," until the effects of your hand make the garden His! Yes, trials, troubles, harsh attacks, and difficulties (persecutions) are part of the life of the believer. Cold kills out the insects which destroy the fruit. Cold hardens the plants so they are not easily bruised and lost. Unpleasantness is a vital part of the experience of any person and merits its place in the growth of the soul. Her demand on the forces of the wind is indicative of the new attitude of the Bride. She commands that which is a necessary ingredient in her growth to happen and by faith calls it into being.

The North winds, however, must one day cease and allow the summer of the soul to take over. In like manner, the South winds are called on to blow on the garden. These soft winds bring green to the surroundings and blossoms to the plants. Fragrances are wafted on their sighs with perfumes so heady any lover finds them favorable. When the fruits of the Bride's labors are evident, then she invites the Bridegroom to take notice and walk among the best.

Personal pronouns change from "my garden" to "his garden," at this point." "Let my beloved come into his garden, and eat his pleasant fruits," is the invitation the Bridegroom has been waiting for. His invitation for her to join Him and come away is matched with "let my beloved come into *His* garden." Preparation has been made for His perusal. Things are in order. She is ready. Without hesitation, He enters the enclosure of her heart and finds such beauty He uses His great "I AM" identification.

"I AM come into my garden, my sister my spouse" is a statement with far reaching implications. For Him to walk in the garden and identify it in the possessive case shows identity with the garden owner. This is Jesus' garden because He is present and possesses ownership privilege. Does this mean the Bride has no power over herself and is dominated by some outsider? No! All along, she has prepared a gift for Him. Her gift is the perfect garden of her own heart. That the gift is given at this particular time in the Song is revelatory.

The scripture declares the day will come when the Lord (the Father) will not be satisfied until He has written

His Law on the heart. It is the garden of the heart where He intends for His Son to dwell. Adam lived in a garden the Lord prepared for Him; the Second Adam lives in the garden of the heart prepared in us. Enclosed and protected, no intruder shall come and bring evil into this garden's gates. No angel with sword of fire will ever be posted in this garden of the heart. This is the Lord's garden, granted Him by one who loves Him enough to make it a wedding gift.

Thousands of years have passed since the first garden, but it has been the plan of God to establish this second since the former was defiled. The book of Hebrews tells us plainly His plan is focused on His Son. Hebrews 10:9,(KJV) says: "He taketh away the first, that he may establish the second." The first garden was defiled and was abandoned; the second garden will have none of this defilement. In one sentence whole epics are displayed when the Bride issues the invitation, "Let my beloved come into his garden and eat." If we are the Bride; let me repeat it; IF WE ARE THE BRIDE: Dwelling in our hearts is the garden, individually, He must accept and desire to walk in and partake of! No fruit is forbidden Him in this "garden of the heart."

This scene has great bearing on all that transpires with the Bride. Her commitment goes to a higher level beginning with this gesture. Her speech earlier, about the "banner of love" being over her, now changes because of this act. She will now be heard to say, "I am my beloved's and he is mine: he feedeth among the lilies (6:3, KJV)." Before the end of the Song, her declaration will change again to, "I am my beloved's, and his desire is toward me (7:10,KJV)." When she gave Him her heart and He received it from her, the timbre of the entire Song changes. No longer will she be the same person she had been. The gift changes the relationship. It means she has reached a place in her relationship where trust, love, and commitment are not words but actions. His receipt of the gift means He owns a part of her that can never be given back. The interchange that takes place here is greater than any consummation in the earthly life. This is covenant. From this garden will come the ingredients He will use in His Priesthood, in the fulfilling of the Old Testament prophecies, and in the marriage supper.

"...I HAVE GATHERED MY MYRHH WITH MY SPICE; I HAVE EATEN MY HONEYCOMB WITH MY HONEY; I HAVE DRUNK MY WINE WITH MY MILK:..."
(SONG 5:1,KJV)

When I declare the Bridegroom will draw ingredients for His Priesthood from the Bride's garden, I do so with candor. I base these conclusions on the couplets which appear in these verses. Solomon again, by the Spirit, uses His knowledge of the Word and his great power as a prophet to affect the scene. Care is taken to use words which are not used in other scripture, to combine words to fulfill scripture, and to group elements which have great significance because of their combination. The first couplet combines the priestly ingredients of myrrh and spice. Remember myrrh is always connected to Jesus. Myrrh was among the gifts of the wise men. Wine mingled with myrrh was rejected (this is important to note) by Him while on the cross. He took the wine vinegar at the very last when it was not mixed with myrrh. Myrrh was used with spices to anoint His body for burial. Look now at the scripture as these elements are used with the possessive "my." Previously, a priest had gathered his spices (or had them gathered) to use in his priestly office. He took them to God and offered them in anointing oils and incense. He gathered them from the earth, and like the animals he sacrificed, they were earthly.

Jesus takes His priestly myrrh and spices from the garden of His Bride's heart. "I have gathered my myrrh, with my spice," He declares. Spiritual? Yes! From our heart come the intercession and prayers before the Lord which are ministered further by our Great High Priest. The only work garnered from our worldly trek (which will be in heaven when we arrive) will be our prayers. It is the prayers of the saints, preserved in vials, which will be opened to perfume God's temple. Our High Priest, who is on a first name basis with us, has gleaned from His garden the ingredients He will mix with His intercession for us. Intercession by Jesus will be a mixture of our heartrending prayer and Spirit groanings and utterances.

When Solomon used the word *basam* (spice), he pointed to the uniqueness of the passage. It is the only time in the Bible this word is used. Surely, he wanted us to know how special were these spices gathered by Jesus.

They will comprise the ingredients of the heavenly incense used in a heavenly temple.

Another couplet is found in this verse: honey and the honeycomb. Again, the personal pronoun speaks worlds. "I have eaten my honeycomb with my honey," the Bridegroom says. Jesus is not unlike mighty Samson who was declared one of the great Faith People in the Hebrews 11 hall of fame. Samson triumphed over the beast and ate the honey and honeycomb from the depths of the Lion. Jesus triumphed over the beast (Satan) by taking away his keys of authority and waits until the earth is his footstool. Jesus spoke not in riddles as did Samson, but He spoke in parables which were as fully frustrating to the Scribes and Pharisees as were Samson's riddles to his enemies.

She (the Bride) who kissed the Rock and had honey and milk on her lips, shares His triumph through association. Her garden yields its resources to Him, and she has them returned by grant of association. When the disciples sat with the resurrected Jesus in Luke 24:42, and literally ate their last meal with Him, He ate the honeycomb (a fulfillment of Song 5:1). He instructed them in the following verses:

> "And they gave him a piece of a broiled fish, and of an honeycomb. And he took it, and did eat before them. And said unto them, **These are the words** which I spake unto you, while I was yet with you, that all things must be fulfilled, which were written in the law of Moses, and in the prophets, and in the psalms, concerning me. Then opened he their understanding, that they might understand the scriptures..."
>
> (Luke 24:43-45 KJV)

Three witnesses were spoken of by Jesus during His conversation: Moses, the prophets, and the psalms. If He had not mentioned the Psalms, I might not have reviewed this set of verses, but He did. How interesting this is. Isaiah 7 says, "He will eat honey." Psalms 10:19 declares the Law, the testimony, the statutes, the commandments, the fear, and the judgments of the Lord are more to be desired than honey and the honeycomb. All these prophecies and pronouncements were satisfied through His sacrifice and now He and His Bride can freely eat of the honey and the honeycomb.

The third couplet is: wine with milk. No doubt a strange combination for mixture, but it is in line with the promise of Luke 24. Her Lover announces to her that from her "heart garden:" "I have drunk my wine with my milk." Few places in the Word combine these two elements. We hear of milk and honey, but rarely do we hear of wine and milk. Quick reference will reveal the vast majority of biblical passages refer to the milk and honey combination. This is all the more reason to lay credence to one of the earliest prophetic passages about Jesus in the Bible: Genesis 49:10ff:

> "The sceptre shall not depart from Judah, nor a lawgiver from between his feet, until Shiloh come; and unto him shall the gathering of the people be. Binding his foal unto the vine, and his ass's colt unto the choice vine; he washed his garments in wine, and his clothes in the blood of grapes: His eyes shall be red with wine, and his teeth white with milk." (KJV)

Isaiah capitalizes on this combination when he declares:

> "Ho, every one that thirsteth, come ye to the waters, and he that hath no money; come ye, buy, and eat; yea, come and buy wine and milk without money and without price." (Isaiah 55:1 KJV)

I believe the wine and milk combination is the Spirit and the Word. The "sincere milk of the Word" is a phrase used by Peter in I Peter 2:2 to indicate the nourishment necessary for the newly born again believer. This "tasting," that the Lord is gracious, works a miracle of grace in the believer's heart, just as the wine of the Spirit does. When the speculators on the street perceived the state of those coming forth from the upper room, they concluded they were drunk. It is Peter who clarifies their state as being filled with the Spirit. Jesus had drunk of that wine (Spirit) like every man must, and His teeth were white from ingesting the milk of the Word, like every man must.

Isaiah says, in the passage we cited earlier, if a person thirsts, his answer is to come to the waters. Jesus used this analogy with the woman at the well and in His great temple pronouncement about rivers flowing from the belly of the believer. Isaiah says those who thirst should buy wine and milk. They are told to buy without money and without price. Wine and milk (Spirit and the Word in combination) must again appear as evidence on the persons who constitute the modern companions of Jesus. This combination will work a work of grace on them like no other combination.

When Jesus spoke of living water to the Samaritan woman, it had no price tag. He said to her he would have "given" it. The wine and the milk have no price tag. They are a part of a new covenant. One of the chief indicators in this testimony to a new covenant is its "free" aspect sealed by wine and milk. Jesus told His disciples they were given their anointing freely and freely should they give. The Bridegroom follows form and issues an invitation to partake freely of all which He enjoys in the garden of His Bride's heart.

In the Song, the Bridegroom invites His companions to partake of the Bride's garden of the heart alongside Him. Like Isaiah, they are told to eat, but only liquids are detailed. They are told to partake in abundance because abundance is characteristic of the kingdom.

"...EAT, O FRIENDS; DRINK, YEA, DRINK ABUNDANTLY, O BELOVED." (SONG 5:1,KJV)

Next, notice the invitation to eat when nothing but liquids are mentioned. Isaiah does the same thing in His 55th chapter. Why would the prophets invite others to eat when wine, milk, and water are all that is offered? I believe there is a spiritual connection here to Jesus' strange statement that unless you ate of Him you would have no life in you.

> "Verily, I say unto you, except we eat the flesh of the Son of man, and drink his blood, ye have no life in you. Whoso eateth my flesh, and drinketh my blood, hath eternal life; and I will raise him up at the last day. For my flesh is meat indeed, and my blood is drink indeed. He that eateth my flesh and drinketh my blood, dwelleth in me, and I in him." (John 6:53-55 KJV)

John continues the mystery further by saying in verse 58:

> "He that eateth this bread (that came from heaven) shall live forever." (KJV)

The Song passage includes all these areas. It presupposes these elements in the garden of the heart (the Bride's garden) must be found in those close to Jesus. It is necessary to eat and drink of those things which they have partaken. It is the Jesus way. To be His disciple, it is necessary to have these elements within.

This "friend's invitation" coincides with Jesus' word to the disciples so closely He calls them not "servants" but "friends." The same invitation is given to all who are in Jesus. All the marvelous gifts bestowed on the Bride, which are found in the epistles, along with the wonderful power given directly from Jesus, plus all the life infilling demonstrations from the Holy Spirit are ready for the taking. The Bridegroom's invitation to his friends to partake of all which He partakes echoes the Isaiah invitation. Jesus must have looked to His Bride when He said, "Yea, drink abundantly, O Beloved." The Bride and the bridegroom share His invitation; they too partake of the same cup. This is why they move and act as one person. They wish all who are His companions to share in the same things, for that is the nature of love. One in the kingdom, one in their commitment, one in their hospitality, one in their faith, one in their baptism becomes the essence of their sharing. Paul teaches this "unity" between the Bride and Jesus. In Ephesians 4:5,6, his treatise is not some ecumenical statement but an echo of that taught in the Song. From their union, the world can come to the springs of blessing and find sustenance. "O Church, drink abundantly!"

Before moving away from the garden scene, it is necessary to observe a few passages in the gospel of Luke. Luke, under the leadership of the Spirit, intersperses some heart garden passages in his accounts of the birth of John and Jesus. Remember when Zechariah named his son John instead of Zechariah? At that moment, he had his tongue of unbelief loosed. The crowd noised this event about Judea. Luke 1:66 says:

"And all they that heard them laid them up in their <u>hearts</u>, saying, What manner of child shall this be!" (KJV)

  Luke 2:19 joins the train of events by relating the action of Mary on hearing the shepherd's testimony. It simply says: "But Mary kept all these things, and pondered them in her <u>heart</u>." Couple this with Mary's reaction after seeing Jesus speaking to the Temple teachers. Luke 2:51 says, "But his mother kept all these sayings in her <u>heart</u>." Each of these major players in the drama of the first coming of Jesus was growing ingredients in their heart-gardens. It is important what you plant in the garden of the heart, for the one who reads the hearts of men may not wish to walk in the midst of what is there. Apart from the planting of a garden in the heart, there are two fundamental truths evident to Solomon: First, the watering of the plantings comes from within; second, a wall or garrison of the heart is absolutely necessary. In Phil 4:7, we find "peace" is the wall. That which does not stand the test of peace must not be planted or allowed to grow. Using this premise, we must cast out fear, unbelief, bad attitudes, troublesome worry, and every aspect of doubt.

  The garden of our hearts must produce the substances which our High Priest can use in His offering of incense. In our heart must be found the living water and the nourishment for those who are to be born in the kingdom. Planted there are the plantings of the Lord, and our heart must be open to the Lord's invitation of review. He must be welcome there. He must find abundance there. He must be able to walk among its plantings and be pleased and overjoyed. His agonizing garden of Gethsemane is no more. His garden of the heart is for His peace. Here is the Eden for the second Adam and His Bride.

CHAPTER EIGHT

TORN VEIL AND STEADFAST HEART

"The watchmen that went about the city found me,..."
(Song 5:7 KJV)

"I OPENED TO MY BELOVED; BUT MY BELOVED HAD WITHDRAWN..." (SONG 5:6,KJV)

Immediately after the King's acceptance and joyful entry into the garden of her heart (now owned by both), the North wind blows a stiff test of the Bride's mettle. Whether the following events are just a dream, as some suggest, or whether they are a prophetic vision, the truths are self evident. The bride has just experienced one of the great spiritual events of her life. Seeking rest from her hosting, she falls asleep, but her heart is awake. The scene which breaks on her is so real it does not seem like a dream. Truths derived from this scene are some of the most cogent for the church in the end time era.

The Bride awakens to hear the voice of her beloved Bridegroom. He, evidently, has parted her company and become involved in some other aspect of His kingdom. Now He returns and knocks, seeking entry; He calls:

"...Open to me, my sister, my love, my dove, my undefiled: for my head is filled with dew, and my locks with the drops of the night."
(Song 5:2 KJV)

His call is unexpected and catches her unprepared (basic training for a call one day when the real event will occur). In her dream, she knows Him by His voice and His endearing words. The stacking of some of these words causes me to think they are words which have grown up between them. Words like "my sister," "my love," "my dove," "my undefiled," point to a composite meaning as well as individual significance. They may have deeper meaning than love phrases between lovers. Significantly, the addition of the term "undefiled" shows she has attained another progressive stage in her spiritual journey.

"...UNDEFILED:..." (SONG 5:2, KJV)

In scripture, the word "undefiled" is used rarely (three times in the Old Testament and four in the New). Song of Solomon accounts for two of the Old Testament renderings and Psalms 119:1 the other.

The Hebrew word for undefiled is *tam*. Only in the Song is this particular word used. The Psalm passage uses a variation: *tamim*. All of its uses in the Old Testament are rendered "perfect, complete, finished." When the Great High Priest of Hebrews 7:26 judges His Bride to be "undefiled," this really calls attention to the word. He who is deemed "holy, innocent, undefiled, and separated from sinners," now passes this trait to His Bride. That is significant!

The Shulamite has traversed from the lowly self-deprecated shepherd girl to one who shares the character and honor of her Lover. She now has the blessing of Psalms 119:1:

> "Blessed are the *undefiled* in the way, who walk in the law of the Lord, Blessed are they that keep his testimonies, and that seek him with the whole heart." (KJV)

She truly has given the King her whole heart, but the ensuing dream sequence will attempt to wrench from her the "undefiled" status. On her very first venture into the world after His pronouncement, she will be challenged in her virginity. The watchmen will seek to defile her.

The New Testament passages related to being "undefiled" are all very spiritual. James declares pure religion (as opposed to the kind of Religion expressed in his day and our own) has an "undefiled" status integral to it. This status expresses itself in action by visiting the fatherless and the widows in their affliction. Compassion is swallowed up in involvement. Platitudes of Religion (characterized by "be ye warmed and filled" or "let them eat cake") are cursed. "Be ye warmed and filled" could have easily been heard from any Pharisee or Rabbi in Jesus' day as he walked past broken humanity. Good Samaritans have the ingredient of involvement which carries a blessing with it. Note the target for involvement is clearly defined:

fatherless and widows in their affliction. However, the definition of pure religion does not stop with action.

To attain the badge of being "undefiled" requires one other aspect, and it is the one thing the modern church does not possess en masse: "keeping himself unspotted from the world (James1:27)." The "undefiled status" is a significant part of the attributes of the Bride. We shall see it in her actions as she eventually joins her lover in service. Still, there is another meaning which must be fathomed in the word "undefiled."

If you follow the root word for "unspotted" in the Greek language, you will discover it has two parts: one part is related to stain; the other part relates to the sea. Let us examine the first meaning: "to stain." If you are in the circle where the splatter falls, you will be stained. If you are near the fallen paint bucket, you more than likely will get spotted. These scenarios produce common knowledge. Every believer knows he cannot hold citizenship in two countries: the stained and the unstained. The world stains, spots, and seeks to put identifying marks on a person's life. That is why in heaven the saints are clothed in white garments; they show readily that they have no stain. His blood cleanses away the stain.

The other meaning (relating to the sea) takes on a different viewpoint. It points to the shore line and the cliffs which are battered by the sea. Inevitably, the winds will cause the waves to batter and tear away the shore line. Inevitably, the world's proximity will, in the same way wear, tear and buffet the believer. It will take its toll. A stained and battered church must seek cleansing and restoration or be viewed as inexcusable.

The modern church is inexcusable. It has no greater leg to stand on than those of the temple in Jesus' day. They cried out, "we are sons of Abraham," but Jesus called them "whited sepulchres full of dead men's bones." He lashed them and turned over their tables. They retaliated with: "crucify Him." The "sons of Abraham crowd" and the "crucify Him crowd" were the same crowd.

Today, churches cry out many things along many fronts. Their range is broad and filled with bragging sometimes as windy as the Pharisees. Jesus says: "show me your 'undefiled' badge." They cry: "away with Him, we have no time for this scrutiny – let us get on with our social programs, our classes, our schools, our outreach ministries and singles groups, our television broadcasts, and our fund raising." Regardless of the denomination or lack of denomination, worldliness has become an integral part of that which must be classified as a "defiled" church. In its present condition, the church is forced to choose to whom it shall minister: to Jesus, or its congregants. No longer are they one and the same. The time has come for the Bride to identify herself by ministering to her "fairest of ten thousand," not her "ten thousand fair ones."

Alas, Ezekiel's sons of Zadok are needed on the scene. They were the only ones allowed to minister to God in Ezekiel's day. The spiritual sons of Zadok will be the only ones who minister unto Him in our day. The sons of Zadok separated the holy from the profane and the clean from the unclean (Ezekiel 44). They taught the people the difference between being holy and acting holy. There was no excuse for remaining defiled. Although their day had sufficient Priests and Levites to carry out the work of the Temple, not one of them qualified. They were "defiled!"

Are we not experiencing similar times? Instead of questioning the professionalism of those who will occupy the pulpit, wouldn't be better to seek the badge of the "undefiled." They may be qualified to minister to the people, but do they qualify to minister unto God? Ministry to the people is a simple task of taking care of need and establishing programs, while ministry to the Bridegroom requires listening to His voice and doing what is said. In like token, ministry to God requires a holy ministration of praise, intercession, and devotion which has few exempla. The Bride must be able to minister to her Bridegroom! Jesus has needs only the Bride can supply. When the Bride is preoccupied with her own needs, there is no time for His. The body must address this issue even while it shouts: "we are the sons of Abraham and the inheritor of all His blessings." How can Jesus share His inheritance with a defiled Bride? If we are to experience I Peter 1:3-4ff, then something must change!

"Blessed be the God and Father of our Lord Jesus Christ, which according to his abundant mercy hath begotten us again unto a lively hope by the resurrection of Jesus Christ from the dead. To an <u>inheritance</u> incorruptible, and *undefiled,* and that fadeth not away, reserved in heaven for you. Who are kept by the power of God through faith unto salvation <u>ready</u> to be revealed in the last time." (KJV)

"...OPEN TO ME...MY HEAD IS FILLED WITH DEW,..."
(SONG 5:2, KJV)

While examining the text, observe the reason for the Bridegroom's return. He says, "For my head is filled with dew, and my locks with the drops of the night (v.2)." Although being damp and wet would be a normal reason for desiring to get away from the elements and into the arms of His loved one, there is more to surmise. In Psalms 110, David talks about Jesus. In verse one, he identifies Jesus, His place at the right of God, and His ultimate victory over the world. In verse two, David speaks of Jesus' power and authority. In verse three, He speaks of His majesty. It is in verse three we find two elements of the Song: morning and dew.

"Thy people shall be willing in the day of thy power, in the beauties of holiness from the womb of the morning: thou hast the dew of thy youth." (KJV)

David gives certain identifying attributes that attend the "day of thy power." On that day there will be a willing people who are fresh with holiness. Uniquely, the scene in which the dew is on Jesus' head is the one showing unwillingness on the Bride's part. (Her attitude, however, will soon change to willingness.) Stranger yet, from this moment forward in the Bride's life, there will never be another act of unwillingness manifested. This is a key turning point in her life. She is not dealing with an ordinary person in ordinary circumstances. She is relating to a King and a Priest, and His call is not an ordinary call to her. His desire for entry is not to escape the night but to share the anointing!

David, further in Psalm 110:4, gives a word-portrait of a priest who resembles Melchizedek. This everlasting priesthood is surrounded by willing people. Holiness (anointing) is on Him like dew on His head (note the dew on Jesus' head in the Song).

Solomon portrays this young Bridegroom (Jesus) wanting entrance to His Bride's presence with the dew of holiness on His head and His locks still dripping from the wetness of it. Jesus expected to find a ready and willing response but disappointedly, turns away from his quest. Why? He knows the door of the heart is opened from within, and He never forces His way into His Bride's life.

In the Shulamite's dream, she gives excuses for not coming to open the door for the King. She gives reasons as flimsy as those used by the ones who could not attend their wedding feast. (From this scene you will understand why those excuses were anathema to them both.) She replies, "I have put off my coat: how shall I put it on? I have washed my feet: how shall I defile them (v.3)?" Put those words another way and they spell, "I'm not ready to see you." "I am busy with my routine and was not expecting to hear from you." "I have gone through ritual cleansing and do not wish to defile myself by touching the unclean." I can hear the church saying, "But Lord, it is night and I've said my prayers and read my Bible and have gone to bed, I'm tired." Notice she alludes her ritual cleansing is the thing that makes her "undefiled." She does not wish to "defile" herself by stepping out onto a "defiling floor." His appraisal of her as being "undefiled" is not a ritual one but based on the condition of her heart garden. Could it be she has not grasped the difference?

Whatever is concluded by the Shulamite's reply, she realizes quickly she has made a mistake. Within a few minutes, she will be out in the street searching for her Bridegroom, and she will only have on her nightgown and will not have on slippers. Somehow, her excuses then will not be acceptable even to her. Whether or not she is prepared, or that she does not wish to be defiled, simply won't make any difference. He is gone, and she wants Him back!

"...MY HANDS DROPPED WITH MYRRH,..."
(SONG 5:5,KJV)

Several events take place between the excuses and the Shulamite's search for the King. These events reveal much about their relationship. When she repents of not giving immediate and unqualified response to His knock, she discovers the door has been affected by His presence.

The anointed One has the anointing on Him. Myrrh covers the knob and evidences of His presence are magnified by its smell. He is the Priest and the smells and ointments of His Priesthood accompany Him. When she touches that anointing, she too has His perfume on her. This is a significant fact!

The Shulamite will soon realize her second visit to the streets is affected by this smell and its identifying perfume. This is in contrast to the world who wants to have the "sweet smell of success" on them rather than the "sweet smelling myrrh" found by being in Jesus' presence. The church must be as concerned about its smell as it is its look. Looking good could be a "white-wash" when the smell it emits is like "dead men's bones."

The Shulamite realizes how the King momentarily thought entrance would be without hesitancy. He expected nothing less. Her heart is moved in compassion for Him and sorrow about her missed opportunity. After all, she has just lost an opportunity to be with Him and enjoy His presence. On finding Him gone, she recognizes a deep-seated principle about Him: He does not force Himself on anyone. His invitation is clear, but there is this other trait as well. (There is coming a day when forceful entry will be His modus operandi, but this is not that day.)

"I OPENED TO MY BELOVED; BUT MY BELOVED HAD WITHDRAWN HIMSELF, AND WAS GONE:..."
(SONG 5:6,KJV)

The Shulamite opens the door too late. Mind you she has just exper-ienced the garden of the heart scene where anything the King wants is her desire. Now she rules her time by her own routine. In the garden, she wants nothing more than to please His every wish. Tonight, she has excused herself and determined her own course. When the beloved withdraws himself, something is wrong. She jumps from her bed and opens the door; she calls for him and briefly looks around for Him. He is gone, and there is no reply. Again, she gives excuse, "My soul failed when he spake (v.6)." Dependence on soul-power will always fail. Soulishness is letting the mind, will, and emotions govern the situation. Soulishness is not what Jesus requires.

Thousands of congregations who claim to be the body of Christ are yet experiencing this scene. Jesus seeks to find entrance to their services, even putting His hand to the door but cannot find entrance. He calls out to open to Him but is met with many excuses. He withdraws Himself, and they realize something is awry. They open to Him on their own time. Realizing He is gone, they frantically search for Him. When He is not readily found, they call out to Him and hear no answer. Their excuse is the same as the Shulamite, "Our souls failed us when He spoke." Jesus has sought to enter their planning committee, their pulpit committee, their social committee, their evangelistic committee, their Sunday Service, their special camps and Bible schools, their retreats and repeats, but they offered one excuse, "Our souls failed us when He spake." Hebrews 12 verse 25 (KJV) says:

> "See that ye refuse not him that speaketh. For if they escaped not who refused him that spake on earth, much more shall not we escape, if we turn away from him that speaketh from heaven."

Let us return to the Shulamite. Her priorities are undergoing a radical change. No longer is it important her feet are unclean, and she is indisposed. Suddenly, the most important thing in her life is being with the King, talking personally to Him, and being close to His touch. Such is the case with those who have experienced Jesus' presence. To be out of fellowship with Him is intolerable. To be in fellowship with Him becomes the chief priority. She must find Him.

Had the Shulamite understood He needs her as badly as she needs Him, she would have remained and prayed for His return. One error often puts a person in the position to cause another. Soulishness is like that! She now decides to find Him by searching. It is her will and determination which after all shall prevail. Sounds reasonable doesn't it? She had established a precedence for this action in a previous situation, and what had worked before must surely work again. Wrong! Rationally, her thinking is correct, but her quest cannot be satisfied through earthly rationality. It does seem "the right thing to do." Her skills at finding him have not diminished since her last quest. After all, she is more committed now than ever. Her commitment will carry her. Wrong! She must have reasoned she was as safe in the street as before, so what harm could come to her now? She gains confidence because the watchmen are there. This, too, is a wrong assumption. (When one tries to venture into spiritual realms without the Spirit's guidance, it is easy to come to wrong conclusions.)

"THE WATCHMEN THAT WENT ABOUT THE CITY, FOUND ME,..." (SONG 5:7,KJV)

Into the street the Shulamite glides with her nightgown pulled tight against her and smelling of the King's myrrh. Her bare feet find the road rough and uneven; it has been a long time since she traversed alone. Let us imagine the events as they may have transpired. She hears someone, so she speaks out, "Who is it? O, it's just the watchman." One of them approaches her and speaks in a surly voice, "What are you doing in the streets with only a nightgown, are you looking for love?" "What are you saying?" she retorts. "No, I am not looking for love...Yes, I know I am dripping with perfume and only have a night gown on, but you are getting the wrong idea!...You are the watchman; you are supposed to protect me from people who would do me harm...What are you doing?...Get your hands off me, you are hurting me....No! I am engaged to the King, can't you see that?...Why do you say I don't look like it?...Get your hands off my clothes!" SLAP! "You hit me! Don't you know who I am?...Wait until the King hears of this...I know He is not here now; I am looking for Him and when I find Him, I will settle with YOU!...Let me go, you monster; you let me go now!...No I don't want to lie with you!...Don't hurt me." POW! POW! "No you will never have your way with me, even if you...." POW!

The Shulamite is knocked down but manages to get up in her wounded state and run, with all her might, to the place she had abandoned before her search. Where else could she find the King except the place where last He visited? Her veil is torn, her arm is bruised, and her body buffeted. She reflects, "I am a mess. How could the watchmen treat me this way? They are supposed to be the guardians against such things in the night, and here they are participating in them."

The scene I have created is completely in line with the scripture. It is in line with reality as well. In the last days, those who are entrusted with the responsibility of guarding the Bride will be the very ones who find her, smite her, wound her, and tear her veil. Why? First, they will not have an understanding of the propensity of their acts. Second, they are so vigorous about their own pursuits, they will not recognize the true Bride. (After all, they did not recognize the Prince of Glory or they would not have crucified Him.) Thirdly, they are the watchmen IN THE WORLD and OF THE WORLD. The world does not recognize Him!

Who are these watchmen? In Jesus' day one of them was the government. The Roman government, under every pledge of constitutional power, should have protected Jesus from that cross but instead empowered it. Religion was a watchman in Jesus' day. Commissioned to be the agent of the Lord on the earth, those of the Temple did not recognize the Son of God.

They sought every opportunity within their power to smite and wound and tear His body and His reputation. Society was an active watchman in Jesus' day. The masses were at peace in an ordered world, but when spiritual things were being done, they called out, "Isn't He the carpenters son?"

The Bride experiences what Jesus' experienced! His enemies were those of His own household. The Bride experiences the often hypocritical hand of those, from counselor to commissioner, from clergy to corporation, from media to merchant, whose first consideration is their own agenda. The true Bride is in for a rough road. The Lord himself declared the days would have to be shortened for the elect's sake.

A torn, wounded, smitten Bride is not a pretty sight! Neither is a self-determined, self-willed, self-effacing one, a pretty sight. The Bridegroom will have neither by His side! He will, however, restore one who comes to the place she left Him last. Crying out to the daughters of Jerusalem, she asks their help in finding her beloved. She has but one message: "I love Him with all my heart."

"WHAT IS THY BELOVED MORE THAN ANOTHER..."
(SONG 5:9, KJV)

The daughters of Jerusalem are quick to respond. They ask the Shulamite an exploring question while predicating their assistance on her answer.

> "What is thy beloved more than another beloved, O thou fairest among women? what is thy beloved more than another beloved, that thou dost so charge us?" (Song 5:9 KJV)

Such a question seems ludicrous at this stage in the relationship. Isn't it evident the Shulamite is hurting and wants her man to comfort her? Isn't it evident she is madly in love with the King and He with her? Isn't it a foredrawn conclusion she is aware of her mistake in attitude and action? Why then is it necessary for her to recount the qualities that make Him so special to her?

Psychologists might have an answer: imprinting. Business managers might refer to the daughter's reasoning as "prioritizing one's goals." Strategists would call it the necessity to "establish value." Counselors and social pathologists would agree such a rehearsal is good for the inner person, hearing herself verbalize. Verbalizing would help her establish a clearer understanding of self and her "significant other." Whatever the reason, the daughters of Jerusalem thought it necessary.

"...HE IS ALTOGETHER LOVELY....
THIS IS MY FRIEND..." (SONG 5:16, KJV)

In answering the question the Shulamaite experiences a "self-realization" which carries her to a surprising conclusion. By jumping to verse 16, you will find she ends her summary of the King by saying in essence, "He is (just) altogether lovely!" She discovers to try to describe all His attributes will take forever. Indeed it will! So, she summarily declares He is everything for which she could hope, plus one other ingredient: He is her friend.

What a discovery! To understand fully this revelation is to have a deep understanding of the Shulamite's position in her Bridegroom. He is her friend. She is not describing someone blinded by romantic love.

She is surveying her situation with Him. They have shared as friends. She knows her best interest is on His heart. She knows He can be relied on. She can tell the most guarded secret, and He will not tell anyone else. She can be herself in His presence without regard to decorum or manners. She can be spontaneous and free and feel no inhibition. She enjoys His company and loves to hear His opinions. They have much in common. She knows He relaxes in Her presence. No amount of stress will overtax their relationship. "He is my friend!" He can arrive at the most inconvenient time, make the most extraordinary requests, and has no qualm in doing so. He can assume special treatment, for He is my friend. Can she describe her friend? Oh, Yes!

The Shulamite's descriptions, from verses 10-16a, are well defined and indicate a knowledge of her lover which she could not have given earlier. She has gotten to know the King intimately, and her word choices make powerful descriptions. What makes them unique is each time she describes a portion of His anatomy, she uses modifiers. These modifiers color and fill. Soon He will express Himself in a similar manner. Juxtapose His descriptions of her and her of Him, and two areas are noted. First, look at the length of the two treatises. His are much more intuitive, subjective, and detailed. Second, both descriptions follow gender lines. She portrays Him as a powerful, youthful male. He portrays her as a beautiful, charming lady.

"MY BELOVED IS WHITE AND RUDDY,..."(SONG 5:10,KJV)

The Shulamite begins by saying her Bridegroom is "white and ruddy." A check of the Hebrew word translated "white" will reveal the word "clear." A ruddy complexion is often used to describe not only a red quality, but a healthy one. A clear attribute could speak to being morally clean. It could be a description of His mental state or the absence of falsehood. To her, He is the epitome of handsomeness and beauty. If she were to pick from ten Thousand, the choice would be Him.

"...THE CHIEFEST AMONG TEN THOUSAND."
(SONG 5:10,KJV)

The first modifier "the chiefest of ten thousand" has been the recipient of much accolade from poets to musicians. Truly, when Jesus returns, He will be at the forefront of multitudes, both of heavenly beings and also earth's saints, past and present. Use of the superlative "chiefest" causes us to ask, "Who are the ten thousand?" Genesis 36 gives a long list of the chiefs (or dukes in the KJV). He is greater than these. Again, in I Chronicles 1:51-54, another extensive list of chief men is noted. He is greater than these. I Chronicles 12 finds another group of chief men being singled out. He is greater than these. He is the "chief" cornerstone which the builders rejected. Although brought before chief priests and rabbis, He conquers them all. He is the image of I Peter 5:4. He is the chief Shepherd. She is correct in her opinion!

Her description is of a youthful man. He is a man possessing power and strength as well as physical beauty and charm. Jesus died in His early thirties. He was a young man. Although rejected and despised of men, and one whose countenance no one desired, He was fairest of all to the one who counts – His Bride.

"HIS HEAD IS AS THE MOST FINE GOLD,... BLACK AS A RAVEN." (SONG 5:11, KJV)

Curly locks and black hair cover a youthful head and are modified either with a crown of gold for kingship or the mitre of a priest. If one could mine the finest gold, it would not be a treasure so great as to be found in the mining of Jesus' thoughts. He is King, but one like Solomon. While walking this earth, He knew the thoughts of men. He reasoned with authority even as a child. He grew in stature and in favor with God and man. Crowned with glory and honor, He stands alone! He is the one who outwitted and out reasoned religious scholarship. He wrapped simple truths into parables only those with spiritual eyes could see. He did not reason like the world; He was spiritually minded. Paul, the apostle, declared: "Let this mind be in you which was also in Christ Jesus (Phil 2:5)." The Shulamite turns from head to eyes in her next treatise.

"HIS EYES ARE AS THE EYES OF DOVES..."
(SONG 5:12, KJV)

The Bridegroom's eyes are like dove's eyes, and this is followed by three modifiers. The dove's eye concept has been discussed as meaning "single of eye." Truly, when Jesus came with the mission of redemption on Him, He was totally focused. He let nothing stand in the way of that plan. No demon could distract Him, no discomfort discourage Him, no group dominate Him, lest He be drawn from the Cross. When He cried, "It is Finished," His eyes were still focused on the empty throne at the right hand of God. The Shulamite's description does not end with focus, for she declares three modifying attributes which characterize His eyes.

The first modifier is "by the rivers of waters." *Aphik,* the Hebrew word used in this context, means "a channel or river bed." Possibly the Shulamite is saying the King's eyes are soft and beautiful like doves residing by a brook or stream. However, I think the reference runs deeper than this. There is an adjectival form of the word *aphik* spelled the same way but meaning "powerful." His eyes were kept focused on the powerful waters. Ezekiel, in his 47th Chapter, testifies of waters which pour out from the throne of God. These are noted to be dividing waters, like those found between two mountains. The eyes of Jesus were focused on the mountain of God beyond the dividing waters. As the waters flowed out from the presence of the Father, so with eyes of compassion, His Being flows to the world.

All these references in this section are about a High Priest. A High Priest had to possess certain physical attributes, and one of them was not to be blemished. He could not be one who was blinded, marred of face, broken of hand, crippled, or dwarfed. Each of the of the body parts she mentions is within the boundaries of the categories of wholeness which must be in a Priest. Additionally, the High Priest is to be married to a virgin and not to a widow or divorced woman. Hence, the virgin Shulamite (Bride) recognizes she is qualified to speak of Him in the most intimate of terms, for she is betrothed to Him. She says He looks like a High Priest with head crowned with gold, face clean and healthy, bearing some of the prominent jewels of the ephod (but bearing them in his body).

Jesus stood at the feast of tabernacles, and just as the drink offering is poured and the water is brought and poured into the vessel and runs forth, He cried, "If any man thirst let Him come to me and drink (John 7:38)." (When

He rose up, He should have been arrested. (The temple guard was obligated to arrest any person who would disrupt the ceremony, but Jesus had such authority they could not.) He resides close to the living water of the Holy Spirit and is ever mindful to fill any man who asks. His eyes are on the true drink offering. His heart is near the wellspring of blessing!

The second modifier, "washed with milk," is a strong indication of the Word within Jesus. Being washed in the Word causes eyes to see differently than non-washed ones. How we look at our fellow man, how we judge our situations, how we walk our path depend on how our eyes have been washed.

The third modifier, "fitly set," not only indicates their position within the facial arrangement, but also is related to Jesus' heart of compassion. Many times the scripture says "He looked upon" something and was moved by what He saw. Whether sheep with no shepherd or Jerusalem in her obstinacy, He viewed them through unique eyes. Paraphrasing II Chronicles 16:9, we observe "The eyes of the Lord run to and fro about the earth in order to show himself strong for those whose heart is perfect." Jesus searches for the perfect heart! He told His disciples if their eyes were single, their whole body would be single (Matt. 6:22). He further instructed them in Matt.13:16, "Blessed are your eyes for they see." He told them if their eye offended them, pluck it out.

The Bridegroom's eyes are set singly. They are full of compassion and washed in the Word. His Bride is deeply moved by His visage. His eyes look on her, and she will not forget how He looks at her. Lovers, whose eyes lock with intensity, communicate more volumes than the printed page.

"HIS CHEEKS ARE AS A BED OF SPICES,..."
(SONG 5:13,KJV)

With cheeks compared with a bed of spices and sweet flowers and with lips like lilies, we are brought face to face with the aura of the Bridegroom's person. The Shulamite uses the modifier of "dropping sweet smelling myrrh" to point to this feature. In the last chapter of Luke,

Jesus appears to His disciples, and they are terrified. He is so kind and calming to them on this occasion He allays all their fear. He offers them to touch Him and see He is flesh and bone even as they. He is human past the resurrection! The Shulamite is emphasizing this fact in her treatise to the daughters. In all the spiritual qualities that are truly his, we must not lose touch of the knowledge that He is human. When we see Him in heaven, His body will be like ours. When He stepped from glory, He did something that could not be undone: He took on flesh, and He still bears the body of a man. Our lover meets us on our level. We are to relate to Him as His Bride.

The smell of myrrh reflects the price Jesus paid and the position He occupies. In all that can be said of Jesus, these two things are foremost: calvary's cross and His righteous throne. They are linked.

"...HIS LIPS LIKE LILIES, DROPPING SWEET SMELLING MYRRH." (SONG 5:13,KJV)

The Shulamite returns to describing her Bridegroom's mouth which can be summarized by saying, "His lips are most sweet." From His lips come words of life, and they are not spoken in commandeering tones. Directed toward the saints, He speaks words of encouragement, words of hope and faith, words like those present at the creation. No foul-mouthed monarch wielding curses on slaves, is this Jesus! A thousand times NO! Here is a Creator, become lover, with one thing in mind: Bringing His Bride Home. (Bring her home with joy in her heart; bring her home with endearments ringing in her ears; bring her home with a mouth like His: "most sweet.") Now, she remembers His hands.

"HIS HANDS ARE AS GOLD RINGS..." (SONG 5:14,KJV)

The Shulamite says her Bridegroom has hands that are like gold rings set with THE beryl. (Because some of my life has been spent in the jewelry industry, I must confess my delight in the illustrative modifiers both these lovers use.) Fineness and strength are relegated in this analogy, along with beauty. Because the article "the" is used in conjunction with beryl, it makes an interesting study. The only references to beryl (which is a topaz and comes in a variety of colors) in the Bible have spiritual connotations.

The breastplate used by the high priest had four rows of stones with three in a row, representing the twelve tribes. The beginning stone of the fourth row was beryl. Each stone was to represent a son of Israel (Jacob).

Another place in the Word where beryl is used is in Ezekiel 28. It is a prophecy against Tyre which includes the stone as descriptive of power. (There are those who believe this to be a reference to Satan when he was in heaven operating as an angel of God while wearing a covering including diamond, sapphire, and beryl) Tyre was cast from a position of power and the beryl stone taken from him.

Daniel 10:6 tells of Daniel's vision with similar descriptions to those of the Shulamite but different in some places.

"His body also was like THE beryl and his face as the appearance of lightning, and his eyes as lamps of fire, and his arms and his feet like in colour to polished brass, and the voice of his words like the voice of a multitude." (KJV)

Further along in Daniel's description, His voice is heard speaking faith and assurance. He also uses the "the" article before beryl.

In Revelation, the foundation stones of heaven find use for beryl. Ezekiel says in his wheel's vision the color of the wheels was like beryl. Whether serving the temple of earth, the realms of heaven, or doing service on the earth, the stone of identity is beryl. Beryl is a heavenly stone. How fitting the Bride recognizes His hands have the anointing of heaven on them. In His earthly ministry, they certainly did.

Look as Jesus places His hands on the sick, the needy, the child, the dead. Observe the tenderness, yet the purposefulness He utilizes. (A man in the healing ministry once told me, he was constantly aware of the presence and power of God that seemed to dwell in His right hand. He made demonstrations laying hands with first the left then the right hand. Remarkable difference was observed. He had witnessed thousands of healings delivered by the laying on of His hands. John Lake had similar circumstances in His ministry.) Imagine the hands of Jesus!

The ephod is not Jesus' priestly identity; His hands are His identifying display. When He did great miracles, it made Him greater than any priest. When He bore our sins on Calvary, it was the nails in His hands and wound in His side which gave Him His credentials. His identifying ephod was His hands, just as gold set with beryl identified the High Priest. The Priest wore an ephod of gold with precious stones representing a chosen people. Those purchased by Jesus own blood are His chosen people. Some allocate the beryl stone in the ephod of the High Priest to be the stone of Asher (happy), and some scholars give it to Benjamin (son of my right hand). Either group would bow before this One who brought joy to whomever His hands touched and now occupies a place as High Priest of heaven.

The linen garments of the Priests were white. The priests' belly was covered with the brilliance of purity. When the Shulamite describes her Beloved, His belly is covered with white as well.

"...HIS BELLY IS AS BRIGHT IVORY..." (SONG 5:14,KJV)

"His belly is white (bright) ivory overlaid with sapphires," reads 5:14b. Again, sapphires are one of the stones of the ephod. Whether assigned to Naphtali or Issachar, the beauty of her portrayal is astounding. The brilliant background, overlaid with dynamic color, is outstanding. Isaiah 54:11 has a key to this verse:

> "O thou afflicted, tossed with tempest, and not comforted, behold I will lay thy stones with fair colours, and lay thy foundations with sapphires..."
> (KJV)

Precious stones adorn Jesus, thus reminding Him constantly of His promise. He takes with Him the reward of them who are afflicted (humbled or lowered) and those who are tossed about (tempest tossed). His belly is the origin of living waters.

Every sapphire description in the Bible has to do with heavenly conjunction. Ezekiel's vision declares the firmament above the throne of God to be like the **sapphire** stone (Ezekiel 1 and 10). Revelations says the foundation-stones of the walls of heaven are decorated with jasper and sapphires. Lamentations 4:7 gives an even deeper meaning to the Shulamite's use:

> "Her Nazarites were purer than snow, they were whiter than milk, they were more ruddy of body than rubies, their polishing was of sapphire:"
> (KJV)

Oh, how the Nazarite of Nazarites must have looked to the Bride; with her lips, she described Him perfectly. Not only does He carry the reward of His promise with Him, but He also stands on strong legs.

"HIS LEGS ARE AS PILLARS OF MARBLE,..."
(SONG 5:15,KJV)

In keeping with the High Priest theme, the Priest must be one whose legs (or walk) are perfect. The Shulamite likens His legs to pillars of marble. Pillars were part of the Temple and were made of wood or brass; however, none of them were noted to be made of marble which raises a question of their use here. The marble is modified with "set upon sockets of fine gold." (Jesus walks in the divine nature.) Just as the Lord gave instructions regarding the Temple and Tabernacle fittings, using rings and sockets, He defines Jesus' legs here. Jesus' legs were not to be broken at Calvary. Jesus' carriage (His legs) were to be stable and dependable, like marble.

"...HIS COUNTENANCE IS AS LEBANON,..."
(SONG 5:15,KJV)

Realizing the Shulamite's next description is tied to the leg profile, one can identify the priestly form. A priest was not to be a dwarf, he was to be of full stature so he would have no difficulty reaching the altar. Her lover satisfies this requirement.

> "His countenance is as Lebanon, excellent as the cedars."
> (KJV)

Surely, the Shulamite is speaking of the priestly office of her King. Excellence is the modifier she uses. He is perfect in all ways and fully qualified to stand in the office of High Priest. She, who witnessed His entree to Her in splendor and recognized His kingship (Song 3:6), now observes Him considering His High Priesthood.

Crescendo is a feeling tone which accompanies the Shulamite's verbal tribute. Beginning at the top of her Bridegroom's head, she offers praise all the way to His feet. (When He begins a similar tribute to His Bride, He begins with her feet and works upward to her head (Song 7:1ff). Crescendo is an appropriate observation regarding the manifesto by which she closes. Beginning with a modest comment at first, she ends with: "He is altogether lovely."

CHAPTER NINE

HE IS NEVER FAR AWAY

"Thou art beautiful O my love..." (Song 6:4 KJV)

"WHITHER IS THY BELOVED GONE,..."(SONG 6:1,KJV)

The daughters of Jerusalem are not asking silly questions; they are intent on having truth imprinted in the Shulamite's heart. In answer to their first question, she has given a graphic portrait of her Beloved and revealed how precious He is to her. Their next question will cause her to have self-revelation regarding a vital truth: <u>He is never far from His Bride.</u> This is a law in the Spirit. God stood separated from His people for many years, but when He sent His Son, the separation was over. The great problem now is to have His chosen ones understand it. Perhaps other cultures have a stronger grasp of this truth than does our own. Maybe different times sensed the presence of Jesus more than our highly centralized, deeply impersonalized information age. (Celtics thought, for instance, that prayer was an ongoing concern, not having beginning or end but permeating the day. All the time, prayer was interwoven into the thread of life in ongoing communion with God.) We live in a time when interest in each other is scheduled, or it doesn't exist. Little do we know of the hovering over, the intense interest in, and the constant provision Jesus has for His Bride. We should know it, for Jesus said that His father is interested in the numbers of our hairs and the sparrows that fall. He is like His Father!

"...WHITHER IS THY BELOVED TURNED ASIDE?..."
(SONG 6:1,KJV)

Perhaps you and I would have recoiled had such a question been put to us. Defensively, we might have answered, "If I knew where He was, I would not be asking you to assist me finding Him." Not the case for the Shulamite, for she accepted what they were doing. Just as she answered their first question from within her inner being, so comes the second answer. He was not "standing in the shadows;" He was in His gardens.

The Shulamite's answer is quick, like "Oh, I know where He must be; He is where He loves to be, in the gardens of the heart." The plural use of garden is to be noted. More than one person makes up the Bride; there are many gardens to inspect, to relish, to enjoy. Jesus is in the "gardens" that open to Him, just as she had done in Chapter 4:16. Can you see the contrast between a closed door and an open garden? Could it be that when we do not respond to His knock, that He departs for other doors?

The Shulamite's answer is without hesitation. She knows where the Bridegroom went, and she will find Him not far away. He is dwelling in the garden hearts of His saints. What a lesson for all to learn. When we have lost the fellowship of the Saviour, a good place to recover the fellowship is to seek out the garden of another saint. No, I am not talking about a cake supper, a single's conference, or a revival meeting. I am talking about acknowledging our error and following the direction of the Spirit until He reveals the Saviour's place of abode. (I have been in services where my need was deep within my being for a renewed closeness, or a touch from God. Then, out of that service, would come some person whom I had not known before, and he or she would stop and give a word from God which was a message from Jesus. Jesus, walking in the garden of that person's heart, used him or her to relate to me: "He is not far away and has you on His mind.")

Jesus is constantly dwelling in the gardens of believers' hearts. He is surrounded by the spices of anointing, for on Him the anointing rests and thus rests within us. He feeds there. Listen Bride; He feeds there! When Jesus said, " I have meat to eat that you know not of," He was giving a great spiritual truth. In the garden of the heart, He is feeding upon the fruit of our yielding. In Revelation, He declares that He will sup with us. How blessed are we that He finds sup within us. How blessed we are to know that His choice place is with us. From the garden of the heart is where the harvest comes. I tell you this great truth: true soul winning is His gathering His lilies from the garden of our heart. Show me a soul winner, and I will show you one who knows this truth. Our mass evangelism may have its place, but it cannot replace the tender spot where grows the sinner yet to be saved – in the garden of a saints' heart. Here the intercession, the careful watering, the tender care issues upon that poor lost soul; until one day, the Great Light draws that soul from the willing soil, and there is rejoicing in the garden.

"...HE FEEDETH AMONG THE LILIES." (SONG 6:3,KJV)

Verse 3 is the culminating answer to the daughters' questions. When the Shulamite issues a confession greater than all the others (but not yet the highest accolade), she says it like this:

> "I am my beloved's and my beloved is mine: he feedeth among the lilies." (KJV)

Two parts are evident in her answer. First, her Bridegroom owns her; second, she owns Him. Would that you and I had complete understanding of her pronouncement. Paraphrased it might sound like this: "I belong to Jesus, and Jesus BELONGS TO ME." She acknowledges that a "meld" has taken place. He has ownership in her life. He has rights within her. Ownership has its privileges! I do not infer the great debate about authority, submission, and understudy that so many churches teach. I do infer the rights of Jesus to the believer's heart. "Why call ye me Lord, Lord, and do not the things which I say? (Luke 6:46, KJV)" is still cogent today.

Conversely, the opposite is true: When we do the things Jesus says, then we have ownership of Him. Does this make an affront to your theology? The Pharisees thought it blasphemy when Jesus claimed to be equal with God. They were sincerely wrong. I tell you, most assuredly, our position in Jesus is one of equality. I tell you it was the intention of Jesus to reign WITH US. I tell you, with authority, we do have rights to Him and on Him. Ownership has its privilege!

When the Bride says, "My beloved is mine," she is revealing one of the highest truths of our day. We are in the last days, and it is important to know what she is saying. Covenant is a two-way street. The Shulamite knows she can ask anything of Him, reveal her inmost heart, or speak to Him about any subject because He will give, understand, and respond. She knows she is not talking to a blank wall or an intangible on a distant shore. She possesses NOW what is to be evident to the world later. How wonderful it is that "He feeds among the lilies." He may not be found in great cathedrals and splendorous halls, but can be found anytime among His own.

HE IS NEVER FAR AWAY

Almost instantly, we hear the Bridegroom's voice: "Thou art beautiful O my love..." It seems as if He has been waiting for His Bride to establish her heart. Once firmly set on Him, He knows no other event will ever separate them. In the Song, the turning point has now been eclipsed. From her, there is a solid commitment to walk beside Him. Gone are the hesitancies to His invitations. With verse 13, comes a willing "yes!" When He cries, "Return, return, O Shulamite," His words are music to her ears. His description of her is unparalleled in scripture.

"THOU ART BEAUTIFUL...AS TIRZAH..." (SONG 6:4KJV)

Three comparisons are used to define the Bride's beauty. Since her beloved compares her to Tirzah, who or what is Tirzah? Tirzah is a city of Ephraim. However, in Joshua 17:3, we find a reference to a "who." When the Promised Land was being divided among Jacob's children, one of Joseph's sons named Manasseh had an unusual circumstance occur. All Manasseh's sons had inheritance through their sons, except Zelophehad who had no sons. On appeal to Eleazar the priest, and Joshua, Zelopphehad's daughters were given equal inheritance with the men.

In an unprecedented act for that day, a woman was granted equal status to a man, both in social status and also in inheritance. Tirzah becomes a figure or archetype of the status of the Bride in Jesus' kingdom. The Bride occupies a position of inheritance ultimately not because society granted it, but the Lord commanded it!

What does this mean? Simply stated, Tirzah was invested with capital and possession she did not earn. Because of her father, she had instant status. She would be capable of making her own decisions within the context of equal power to others who stood in inheritance. This is truly the Bride of Jesus. Born into the kingdom through the new birth and now come to maturity, she is the inheritor of that which she did not earn and invested with wealth and status for which she did not labor. Her decisions are based on love and not from a sense of obligation. Her marriage is based on her will, her choice. These qualities make the Bride as beautiful as Tirzah.

"...COMELY AS JERUSALEM,..." (SONG 6:4,KJV)

The Bridegroom's second qualifier is also a city. The Bride is as "comely as Jerusalem." No city on earth is more revered or as loved as this city. To be compared to Jerusalem is the highest of compliments. Jerusalem is a city of promise, prophecy, and protection. Although Jerusalem has experienced excruciating pain, it keeps birthing life and is truly the "Holy City." Judgment has fallen on its children, but covenant promise has lifted them up. Its peace is the object of blessed prayers. The cry of Jesus, heard above its din, was: "O Jerusalem, Jerusalem, how oft would I have gathered you like a hen doth her brood, but you would not (Matt.23: 37)." We see Jesus weep when He beholds her "situation," for she stood beautifully on the mountains. In His wisdom, He knew her destiny. No city on earth looks, feels, or touches the emotions of so many people as Jerusalem. This city, where all the nations of earth will one day be judged, has the ignominy of Calvary and the promise of glory. The Shulamite (Bride) reminds Him of both events. Jesus died in order for her to have future glory.

Those who are the Bride will find heaven coming to them just as Jerusalem will have heaven rest on it. Judgment is on those who mistreat the Bride, just as there is judgment on those who mistreat Jerusalem. Solomon saw Jerusalem in its zenith, and for him to compare the Shulamite to its beauty is superlative par excellence. The Temple was its crowning glory, and His Temple in the heart of the Bride is Jesus' crowning glory. Early in this treatise I said the Song and Revelation were linked; this is one of those places. In Revelation 21:9-10, we read:

> "And there came unto me one of the seven angels which had the seven vials full of the seven last plagues, and talked with me, saying, Come hither, I will shew thee the BRIDE, the Lamb's WIFE. And he carried me away in the spirit to a great and

high mountain, and shewed me that great city, the holy Jerusalem, descending out of heaven from God." (KJV)

The link between the Bride and Jerusalem is solidified in these verses. Solomon has not randomly chosen his comparison of the Shulamite to the comeliness of Jerusalem. He is showing the link that is already established and looking far ahead revealed it.

"...TERRIBLE AS AN ARMY WITH BANNERS."
(SONG 6:4, KJV)

The last qualifier in this series is an army with banners. The Bride is compared with an "awe inspiring" scene. An army with banners flying and victory on their mind is, indeed, an awesome sight. This is a scene for the last days. The church has never been truly viewed with its banners flying while approaching the gates of a hell that are unable to resist her. Three thousand years ago, Solomon saw such a Bride! For years the church has sung about Christian soldiers, but a fully equipped, armor clad, banner flying, body of believers with the mind-set to rescue the multitudes from hell have not been seen. She has been prophesied by Solomon and will be seen on the earth! The Hebrew word for armies (*dagal*) is used here and only here, and it means "to carry and lift up a standard."

"So shall they fear the name of the Lord from the west, and his glory from the rising of the sun. When the enemy shall come in like a flood, the Spirit of the Lord shall lift up a standard against him." (Isaiah 59:19 KJV)

"TURN AWAY THINE EYES FROM ME, FOR THEY HAVE OVERCOME ME:..." (SONG 6:5, KJV)

In verse 5, I believe Solomon uses a play on words. He uses the Hebrew word *RAHAB* (overcome). The verse opens with a request for His Bride to turn away her eyes. I believe she has focused on Him with such intensity she disturbs Him. She is not taking her eyes off Him, for she has found Him and does not want to let Him out of her sight! Marginal notes will take the phrase "for they have overcome me" and point to *rahab* as being "puffed." It can mean "proud or strengthened." If the last duo is true, then

He is saying, "Your eyes have strengthened my belief in you." Perhaps He is saying, "You make me proud when I look into your eyes, for they tell me how intense is your love." Because Solomon uses the word *rahab* to produce the word "overcome," I believe He is saying more. It is like "you have *Rahab*(ed) me." Taking license, I would offer this next sentence: "When I look on you, I am as overwhelmed as Israel in their being saved by Rahab." Israel could not have imagined God would use such a person as a harlot to house and ultimately protect them. She, in turn, was saved by them. Having received a promise based on her faith, she was saved out of a "soon to be destroyed" society. Israel saw Rahab, the undeserving, made to be deserving through faith. The Bride is made up of those who, through faith, have found grace. Coming forth from the "soon to be destroyed society," she reminds Him of faith-filled Rahab. Although she was not born into Israel's family, she is of Abraham by faith.

"...THY HAIR..." (SONG 6: 5, KJV)

The translators do a strange punctuation as this point, they put a colon not a semi-colon, meaning everything that follows is somehow connected. This keeps the reader from disconnecting the Rahab concept from all the rest. The Bridegroom is overcome with all the Bride's beauty. Every feature raises the pitch of intensity of His love for her. (Note I said His love for her.) Jesus is dynamic. His love is dynamic. As He is timeless now, the expression of love is timeless now. Historically, His death had not taken place when the Song was written. Futuristically, it has already taken place, and He is viewing His Bride in light of the love shown at Calvary. His love is ever continuing on a continuum of NOW. He died on the cross for her. Now, beholding her, He is overcome with love. So, before Him is the object of all the pain, struggle, and suffering; she is beautiful! She is worth the saving! She stands as redeemed as Rahab, who was triumphant through her faith! (In Revelation, we accept the intermingling of past, present, and future. The same must hold true for the Song.)

"THY TEETH..." (SONG 6:6, KJV)

Continuing the series, the Bridegroom uses illustrative terms which are consistent with His previous love couplets, such as hair and Gilead (see previous comments). When He says the Bride's teeth are as a flock of sheep, He speaks of "white and even." His remarks about temples or cheeks like pomegranates have been part of his previous love terms. The emphasis is clear; He does not think of her in diminution because of her former trials. His appraisal stands! His opinion remains consistent. She is more beautiful because of her trials! He refers to sheep going up from the washing. He has washed her in His blood! He refers to them being like twins, which is duplication in kind. Her duplication in kind will turn into multitudes! What she endured at the hands of the watchmen and the agony of her search has made her more determined than ever to follow Him. Many of the multitudes of heaven came forth from great persecution and tribulation, just like the Shulamite. Their separation is over. The Bride will not be separated from Him ever again and that thought draws Him. She remains the woman with a history of sacrifice, washed by the blood, and having a mind fertile with the Word. There is no barrenness with her; barrenness is foreign to their relationship! (The pomegranates between her locks also speaks of fertility of mind.) She is bubbling over with fruitfulness from every sector of her being!

Because of the punctuating colon, we must add the phrase "turn away" to the Bride's hair, her teeth, her cheeks just as we have with her eyes. When love is vibrant, the sight of hair, of a smile, of a glowing demeanor is just as evocative to emotion as are eyes.

"THERE ARE THREESCORE QUEENS,..."(SONG 6:8,KJV)

Notice the Bridegroom stops for the moment. Instead of continuing the descriptions of chapter 4, He shifts back to chapter 3 and draws on it. In Chapter 3, we saw 60 mighty warriors surrounding Jesus, who is the mightiest of warriors. He is the chief Warrior! Now, apparently, He is ready to show the Bride her true identity in much the same way. Surrounded in like manner with those of rank, she outranks them all. Again the number sixty[1] is used but now in connection with Queens. I believe He uses "Queens" to refer to Israel in the same manner as the

---

[1] Another was of looking at this is that 60 = 5 X 12. Five is the number representing grace and twelve represents divine order or divine government. Therefore sixty also means that God will bring about divine government (Theocracy) by His Grace (by His Power).

"warriors" of chapter 3. As was shown in the previous discussion, sixty has to do with an arrangement of tribes without Judah and Levi. Note the following change: These are Queens and not warriors. Look into Revelation 12 where one woman represents all Israel (the true Church past and present) in the birth of the many-membered body of Christ (of which Jesus is the head). As Mary was the mortal vehicle used to birth Jesus, she was an archetype of all Israel. So, in fact, Israel gave birth to the Saviour and acted as Queen. Ranking higher than the concubines, they are the chosen people. True Israel serves in the office of a Queen, reigning as the fertile mother, pregnant with the Word, and giving birth to The Word.

Conjointly there is a depiction of 80 concubines. Although concubinage throughout the Old Testament was sanctioned, we must ask its place here. I believe the concubines represent the nations of the world which, although they were not Queens, have served their purpose in the will of God and His plan for the ages. Concubines bore children of destiny to patriarchs of old. So the nations of the world have born their men of destiny.

"Virgins without number" represent the untold thousands who are the saints making up the total body of believers. Those even yet to be born into the kingdom are here represented. They are massed together as in Revelation where thousands upon thousands surround the throne and sing a new song. These are the redeemed, the restored, those with the white robes.

"MY DOVE, MY UNDEFILED IS BUT ONE;..."
(SONG 6:9, KJV)

Turning to His beloved the Bridegroom now bestows on her the power of her position. Just as a lover presents His beloved to His friends, He presents her to these contemporaries. "My dove, my undefiled is but one," is like saying to a room full of adorers, "she is the most beautiful woman in the world. She is the only one." Clearly, she is His choice for a Bride. "Holiness" can be interchanged for the word "undefiled" in this rendering. "Perfect" and "finished" are two other meanings. Let Believers be warned, the worldliness accepted by churches and congregations as being normal is not! The finished work of the Word is complete in His Bride. She is undefiled! He points it out by saying in essence: she is rare ("is but one") She stands out as the "choice one of her that bare her." The "many called" but "few chosen" scripture has application here. Jesus is not Jacob. His Bride is the "only one of her mother." "She was created for me," might be a good translation. Nevertheless, the daughters of Jerusalem saw her and "blessed" her. The queens and the concubines praised her. In this instance, she is <u>identified</u> with the King. The praise and blessing that come to Him now come to her. She is getting a glimpse of what is in store for her. She is able to see herself as the one who, through overcoming faith and the attonement of Calvary, is able to receive praise and blessing. We must, as the Bride, become accustomed to this praise as we "sit together in heavenly places" with Him.

"...FAIR AS THE MOON, CLEAR AS THE SUN,..."
(SONG 6:10,KJV)

This "overcomer" Queen begins to hear greater accolades than she has before. Was it not enough to have heard what has just coursed the Bridegroom's lips? He refuses to stop this torrent of praise. He loves her! "Who is she that looketh forth as the morning?" He calls. This is a "new day" comment. Just as the new day holds the promise of adventure and new blessings, she looks forward to His day. The Hebrew word *shachar,* translated "morning," can be translated "dayspring" or "early morning." By connecting I Peter 1:19 to this verse, we get a clearer picture:

> "We have also a more sure word of prophecy whereunto ye do well that ye take heed as unto a light that shineth in a dark place, until the day dawn, and the day star arise in your heart."
> (KJV)

This lady has let the daystar arise in her heart! Beyond this, she is the reflection of the Sun (Son). "Fair as the moon," connotes her position in Him. Her light comes from Him! "Clear as the Sun," depicts truth working in Her making her shine like Him. He is the light of the world, His light is in her, and she is letting their light shine in the darkness. "Terrible as an army with banners," reiterates the truth of the former passage. A graphic of the Bride is beginning to emerge. She is a woman of the finished work, shining in victory, and surrounded by glory. As the sun is the glory of the day, so the moon is the glory of the night.

Her glory is derived from her proximity to Him and shall grow and grow until:

> "... the light of the moon shall be as the light of the sun, and the light of the sun shall be sevenfold, as the light of seven days, in the day that the LORD bindeth up the breach of his people, and healeth the stroke of their wound." (Isaiah 30:26 KJV)

"I WENT DOWN TO THE GARDEN..." (SONG 6:11,KJV)

Reference to the Bridegroom's going down to the "garden" is significant enough to point to her fruitfulness. He went into her spirit garden and inspected the "nuts" (Hebrew word: *egoz*). The "nut" is a fruit which is obtained by going through an outer shell. The Word pierces through the flesh and enters the human heart. It is the human heart, covered by flesh, where the issues in life come forth. When He looks into her heart, he finds her vine flourishes and her pomegranates are budded! The irresoluteness that manifested itself in her past is clearly gone. She is single-minded, single-visioned, and sold out in her devotion to Him. It is well with her soul!

"...MY SOUL MADE ME LIKE THE CHARIOTS OF AMMINADIB." (SONG 6:12,KJV)

Verse 12 is covered with descriptors. Center references cannot wait to tell the reader the translators did not know fully how to handle this passage. Understandably, the translators had difficulty in finding a true meaning for this verse; their focus was on the wrong area. Let us survey the passage. First, delete the italicized word "like" as it was put there for clarity in the King James Version. Next, take the name Amminadib, and recognize the variant to the name Amminadab. *Amminadab* is a Hebrew word for "my willing people," which explains the center reference in many Bibles. The word *Amminadib* is different. Only used in the Song, and no where else in the Word, this word is translated: "a willing, generous, prompt, liberal people." I believe Jesus is the one doing the talking here. I believe He is saying, "before I knew it, my soul made me the chariots (or vehicle) of a willing, generous, prompt, liberal people. These people were free (as in free, open to suggestion, progressive, not bound by traditional or conventional ideas, abundant). Yes, when you get among fruit bearers (the folks with the budding pomegranates), you find they are your kind of folks. They are not bound up in traditional religion or conventional ideas but are free flowing in the Spirit and liberal in their giving. They are free! Their minds are open to the slightest suggestion of the King. They move without hesitation. They are the ones who live in abundance. They are free indeed! Our Jesus told his disciples, "the truth will make you free." The very soul of Jesus is the vehicle for those who are free!

"RETURN, RETURN, O SHULAMITE;..." (SONG 6:13,KJV)

Verse 13 in the KJV is verse one of Chapter 7 in the Hebrew text. The difference in division is based on a matter of focus. If you have the daughters of Jerusalem speaking versus the Bridegroom, then you tend to shift the verse. I tend to split the action. I have the Bridegroom calling to her in multiple form, echoed by the daughters in multiple form. He calls her to return, or to come to Him, thus signaling it doesn't matter that she made a mistake in not answering His call. It only matters that she is beside Him.

The text translators have placed a semicolon at the end of the first burst. The echo begins with "return, return, that we may look upon thee." What the daughters see is a woman full of the attributes which Jesus has just described. They affirm they see in her "the company of two armies." He has been more modest than they. Their use of terms is unique to this setting. Actually, they portray her as dancing between two armies rather than being like two armies. In this sense, they coincide with His appraisal. She is like an army within an army. *Mahanaim* meaning "to dance" is transliterated in the Amplified Bible. It leads to a study of the meaning in Hebrew which can be several things: encampment, army, host, troop, band, or station of priests. If you take the last meaning and have her dancing between two stations of priests, you will have my understanding of the verse. Here is a free and liberated Bride dancing in the midst of the Priests. That is how I see the church: filled with the Holy Spirit, dancing freely among the priests. We are kings and priests unto our God. The Bride stands boldly, as an army with banners, but free and liberated to dance without shame (like David) between the Priests. She should be prepared, however, for the same criticism David received and be ready to give the same response. David did not receive the criticism into His spirit but danced harder!

CHAPTER TEN

THE PRINCE'S DAUGHTER

*"How beautiful are thy feet with shoes,
O Prince's daughter"* (Song 7:1 KJV)

NEW DESCRIPTIONS FOR A NEW LADY

Is the Bride elevated to the station of a "Prince's daughter" as an irrelevant love statement or is this the same Shulamite who was formerly defined as a shepherd girl? True, she has come a long way from the days among the goats in the Judean Hills. Solomon chose this moment to show her complete change. She is changed to the Bride of equal stature with Him. A "Prince's daughter" would be a good choice for a King's mate. A "Prince's daughter" would have the station, ability, equal background, and the social graces to fit well into the society of His Lordship. No, Solomon does not have the King of Kings saying such lofty words to ingratiate a paramour. He speaks the truth, and this truth is sure: From this point on in the time of the Song, she will stand as His equal. From this chapter forward, beginning with verse 12, the "I or Me" is changed to "us."

A passage in the Psalms draws attention to this portion of the Song. Psalms 45 opens with a description of a mighty King who definitely is Jesus, "Thy throne, O God is for ever and ever: the sceptre of thy kingdom is a right sceptre." Following these identifying remarks a female is described:

> "King's daughters were among thy honorable women: upon thy right hand did stand the queen in gold of Ophir. Hearken O daughter, and consider and incline thine ear; forget also thine own people, and thy <u>father's house</u>; So shall the king greatly desire thy beauty: for he is thy Lord; and worship thou him. And the daughter of Tyre shall be with a gift; the rich among the people shall intreat thy favour. The King's daughter is all glorious WITHIN: her clothing is of wrought gold. She shall be brought unto the king in raiment of

needlework: the virgins her companions that follow her shall be brought unto thee. With gladness and rejoicing shall they be brought: they shall enter into the king's palace. Instead of thy <u>fathers</u> shall be thy <u>children</u>, who thou mayest make <u>princes</u> in all the earth. I will make thy name to be remembered in all generations: therefore shall the people praise thee for ever and ever.

(Psalms 45:9-17 KJV)

With this passage in the forefront, light is shed on these opening verses of Song chapter 7. The King is describing one who is not to consider her earthly parentage, position, or inheritance but her new self. She is described as one who is glorious "within." From Psalms 45, we glimpse her garments and glory.

"HOW BEAUTIFUL ARE THY FEET WITH SHOES, O PRINCE'S DAUGHTER!..." (SONG 7:1,KJV)

The Song follows the same pattern as the Psalms passage, identifying the Bride first as a "Prince's daughter." We then look at her in the same light as the Psalms passage. All we hear from Jesus' lips must now be predicated by the fact He is describing a "new woman." She is still the Shulamite, but the Shulamite made into a new creation. She is now a "Prince's daughter" because she is born of God and has come to maturity. No metamorphosis is greater than the character and life change that comes through this birth. The Bride has been growing in wisdom which has culminated in His appraisal the "time has arrived." He describes her in new terms, in glorious terms, which eclipse His former words. Her attributes are magnified in Chapter 7.

"How beautiful are thy feet with shoes," says the King in His opening lines. Already we know He is ranging his comments from His Bride's feet to her head. He has reason for this. Not only is He building crescendo, but also His purpose is much more profound; it is spiritual. From this first comment, He is drawing attention away from the physical to the spiritual. She has on shoes. Note the words of Jesus to His disciples when he first sent them out. They were not to take script, coat, or shoes. One of the marks of their estate was to be shoeless. Most Biblical references to shoes call for the removal of them rather than specifically calling attention to wearing them. Once, Ezekiel was told to put on his shoes; it was at the death of His wife (symbolic of the death of the flesh). Specifying he wear his shoes must have had significance. It must have been irregular behavior for such a time of grief. Ezekiel's shoes drew attention to a deeper meaning God wished to convey.

John the Baptist said of Jesus, "I am not worthy to unlatch His shoes." Romans 10:15 says, "How beautiful are the feet of them that preach the gospel." All these references dim when compared with a mighty speech God made to Israel in Ezekiel 16. He told Israel she was like an exposed child polluted in her own blood when He found her. He tells how He loved her, cared for her, nurtured her, and hovered about her until she grew up. He treated her like a woman of rank and station. He clothed her in gold and embroidered work. He <u>shod</u> her with badger's skin and girded her with fine linen. He bedecked her with ornaments of chains and bracelets. (Notice He specifies badger skin shoes.) He was disappointed in her, though. She turned from Him and played the harlot after being proclaimed the most beautiful among the nations. She trusted in her beauty. This will not happen with Jesus' Bride.

Too many parallels are in these two passages to ignore them. Jesus' Bride is adorned with shoes, but she is faithful. She trusts not in her beauty. She is the finished work, not the beginning work, for she wears her shoes. (The disciples represented the beginning work when they were sent forth with no shoes.) Her feet are "shod with the preparation of the gospel of peace." How important to understand Solomon (Jesus) is speaking spiritual truths. The beauty of His wife is renowned. Her love for Him is also renowned.

"...THE JOINTS OF THY THIGHS ARE LIKE JEWELS,..."
(SONG 7:1, KJV)

Those who seek erotic meaning from these verses must also look at the erotic allusions that could be applied to the Ezekiel passage as well. To interpret the Song differently from Ezekiel is amiss. The next verses about her navel and breasts might well lend themselves to an erotic interpretation but not considering the total picture. Why is it necessary to draw attention to her thighs?

(Jeweled movement watches run well, so do thighs which are like jewels.) Here, the Hebrew word *chali* may mean jewels or ornaments. Notice it is the joints of her thighs which are like ornaments. Remember a famous thigh in history that an angel put out of joint? Jacob's (Israel's) limp was from an out of joint thigh which was a constant sign of his wrestling with God. The Bride's thighs are not out of joint but are jeweled. Her walk is perfect.

In Numbers 5, the priest performed an unusual rite of jealousy which involved a woman's thighs. A woman, questioned as to her faithfulness in marriage, was obliged to drink a potion which determined her innocence or her guilt. If guilty, a curse was placed on her. The curse was that her belly would swell and her thighs would rot. No rotten thighs with this Bride! The joints of her thighs are like jewels, fitly placed. How significant is this "thigh" passage? Very! On Jesus' thigh is an insignia: "King of Kings and Lord of Lord's." On her thigh is an insignia: jewels reminding the world of her faithfulness. Such a description shows "fineness" as well. He is saying in the total speech, "Look at this fine lady, beautiful in her own right and made more beautiful by my love."

"THY NAVEL IS LIKE A ROUND GOBLET,..."
(SONG 7:2,KJV)

Her navel, which mostly refers to life, is next in the sequence of praise. The uncut birth cord was a sign of rejection and castigation in ancient days. Not so with the Bride, for she is no castaway. She has heeded Proverbs 3:8. She has acknowledged the Lord in all her ways and bears the reward. The promise, "It shall be health to thy navel and marrow to thy bones," is exemplified in her. She is full of life and spiritual wisdom.

"THY TWO BREASTS ARE LIKE TWO YOUNG ROES..."
(SONG7:3,KJV)

The Bride's breasts, the place of nurture and life (to future children), are beautifully described. By emphasizing her breasts, Solomon alludes to other scripture which also emphasizes the breast. Look at Genesis 49. When Jacob gathered his sons to him, he prophesied about the last days. To each child he gave a specific word. When he came to Joseph, he gave a special blessing. In verse 25 we see that blessing:

> "Even by the God of thy father, who shall help thee; and by the Almighty, who shall bless thee with blessings of heaven above, blessings of the deep that lieth under, <u>blessings of the breasts</u> and of the womb." (KJV)

Is not Jesus more blessed than Joseph? Is this not a refinement by person of the words of Proverbs 5:18ff:

> "Let thy fountain be blessed: and rejoice with the wife of thy youth, Let her be as the <u>loving hind and pleasantroe</u>; let her *breasts* satisfy thee at all times; and be thou ravished always with her love." (KJV)

Every aspect pointed out about breasts found in the Proverbs' passage is found in the Song passage. Her breasts are like the roe, and they are the focal point which sets her apart from all others. She alone is to be the object of His affection. He is to be "ravished by her love." He is!

"THY NECK IS AS A TOWER OF IVORY;..."(SONG 7:4,KJV)

In Psalms 45:8, reference is made to ivory palaces, but this word translated tower is actually temple. Temples, or towers, were built in old days to show stability and strength. A tower signified a land occupied with enough peace to cause the owner to build improvements and enhancements to the beauty of the landscape. The Bride is now at rest in the Bridegroom, and the tower of her neck is proof she will be with Him forever. He has invested in her, for there is peace within her borders. She is permanent.

"...THINE EYES LIKE THE FISHPOOLS IN HESHBON,..."
(SONG 7:4,KJV)

In this passage the Bride's eyes are not described as dove's eyes as in former words. Her eyes are like the "fishpools of Heshbon by the gate of Bathrabbim." Uniquely, these words are not common to any passage in the Bible but the Song. *Heshbon* means "stronghold." *Bathrabbim* means, "daughter of many." Fishpools are references to two pools which were fitly placed at the entrance to the gate of the city. As the name would imply, they had live fish beneath the surface. Enhancing the landscape of the city gate, these pools were reprieves of beauty and relaxation. Her eyes were resorts of beauty and relaxation. Literature is rife with men who have been attracted by the eyes of a woman. Human senses have often been referred to as "gates" (ie: the eye gate, ear gate, etc.). This daughter, who is the composite of many, has beautifully set eyes where life abounds beneath their surface. Her eyes are strongholds of faith, guarding her inner person from the intrusion of sin. Yes, she has dove's eyes, too.

...THY NOSE IS AS THE TOWER OF LEBANON...
(SONG 7:4,KJV)

The Bride's nose "as the tower of Lebanon" makes reference to beauty "in place." Again, the nose of the High Priest must not be broken. Hers is not. Even as Solomon built buildings in Lebanon, he no doubt built towers there as well. Because of the addition "which looketh toward Damascus," I believe both He and the Shulamite knew the exact tower. I believe in the mind of Solomon, there was no more beautiful tower than this one. He is complimenting her perfection and uniqueness.

"THINE HEAD UPON THEE IS LIKE CARMEL..."
(SONG 7:5,KJV)

Her head is like Mt. Carmel (a place where the false gods were put down and the fire of God prevailed). Is this not true of the Bride? Has she not challenged every thought and every concept that assaults the Word? Has she not brought every thought under the Lordship of Jesus?

...THE HAIR OF THINE HEAD IS PURPLE
(OR CRIMSON);..." (SONG 7:5,KJV)

The Bride's hair reflects the crimson of Calvary. Her covering is Jesus' blood. The Bride is constantly "covered" by pleading the blood. How beautiful she looks to Him in that covering. How drawn He is to giving all she desires. He is "held in their galleries" (meaning ringlets or flowing). He is held by that which flows from her presence. He is captured, for she is fair and pleasant. She has won His heart.

Listen saints; we have the attention of our Jesus. He wants to hold us next to Him, speak loving words into our midst, and be blessed by all He sees. Would the whole body of believers could see holiness pays. Would we could see ourselves as He sees us. He sees us according to what we must become. Listen, He is talking to us even as Solomon spoke to the Shulamite. He is explaining in detail the things of beauty He wants in us. He is setting before us the prime example. To become what He sees in us must be our constant goal. Such should be our aim always, but alas, we have lost sight. We need an Ezekiel to show the "Church to the church." We must not be a repetition of history. We have no options. We shall not be a disappointment to Him. We shall not savor His good things and walk in our own ways. The portrait is already painted in the Song. This is the way we shall look, or we shall not stand beside Him!

"HOW FAIR AND HOW PLEASANT ART THOU,..."
(SONG 7:6, KJV)

Three words are modifiers in the Bridegroom's next plethora of praise. The first is "fair," which is the Hebrew word *yaphah*. Used in the Song and in Ezekiel, its imagery is sublime. In Ezekiel, the prophet describes the beauty of a tree, so beautiful all the other trees in the garden of God envied it. The Bride is so beautiful all who behold her are envious. I believe when the Religions of this world behold the true Bride and know they are not like her, they will be jealous and envious.

The second modifier is "pleasant." In English, this word has little power. "Pleasant" has a neutral connotation often used to describe something less than dynamic. It is not so in the Song! Only five times in the Word is this term coined—four with positive and one with negative meaning. None of the occasions lack power and fire. The most significant passage for study is II Samuel 1:26, when David mourns the death of Jonathan:

> "I am distressed for thee, my brother Jonathan: very <u>pleasant</u> hast thou been unto me: thy love to me was wonderful, passing the love of women."
> (KJV)

In this passage the word "pleasant" has fire. United with wonderful, its meaning reaches into the Song and to the Shulamite. She is a woman, and her love has reached into Him more strongly than the love of David and Jonathan. Pleasant (*naam*) is now a term of preciousness. Between David and Jonathan, it signifies all the unspoken avenues explored by a "covenant brother." It carries the memory of a friendship in which no secret is too deep to be revealed.

Naam is filled with passion when viewed considering special "covenant" vows and pledges. The "blood covenant" between David and Jonathan was a far reaching pact. Those familiar with covenants in the Old Testament days know the cross promises which bound the individuals involved even into future generations. (Those unfamiliar with covenants of blood between people in the Old Testament should make a careful study of the primary pacts covered in them.) The Bride is the repository of a "covenant" relationship.

The third modifier in this verse is the word "delights." Hebrew lexicography records the form *taanug* only three times in scripture. All three appear in Solomon's writings. It can be translated "delicate or luxurious." Delicate carries with it terms like choice, elegant, exquisite, fine, delightful, and select. "Fragility" also holds an integral part in this passage but only in relation to showing "sensitivity and skill in dealing with others or the ability to detect effects of great subtlety or precision." A matter being of a fragile nature might incorporate feelings or emotions as well. "Luxuriousness" is a definition of delight. It means something is "more than excessive." It can be interpreted as "magnificent, majestic, or stately." These terms are carefully chosen to show a woman who has arrived at her place of status and position. She rules with sensitivity to others and in a noble manner. When you consider to whom she is joined, you are positive He ensures she has excess.

Solomon's shift in these descriptive areas is to introduce us to the Bride who will carry us through to the end of the text and into eternity. Beginning with her newly defined identity, He turns to fine-tune our understanding of her. This is the woman to be embraced forever by the King of Glory. It is important to see her as He sees her. She is whom we are becoming. It is like looking at the finished person while still in the creative process. She is our pattern, our very essence, of which we will be a part. We shall reflect every attribute of her as we become His Bride.

It is this Bride who will soon accompany Jesus into a new dimension of glory. They will turn away from themselves and begin to minister to others, and their concerns will broaden. She will think as He thinks, look on situations as He looks, and discern with His discernment. Grace is the hallmark of her existence. She has discovered the futility of flesh and self-seeking. Total grace and nothing more constitutes the fiber of her being.

Throughout her journey in the Song, the Bride has learned to confess that without Him she is nothing. She has acknowledged her need for His healing, for she has wearied of stumbling. In the next verses the reader will comprehend her change. She begins to act on His grace. She moves out on the assurance His finished work is indeed complete within her. Now He can blend exquisitely with her.

DELICATE LADY/DELICATE MAN

To appreciate certain qualities in another person, some possession of those qualities must appear as very important to the person commenting. Reflexive as this may sound, it is true. Pay attention to the many facets of fineness expressed, and learn how they relate to both. For example, the qualities of spiritual discernment found in the Bride are also found in the Bridegroom. As He admires qualities in her, these elements are what He finds pleasing. She has become all His prophetic expressions have pointed to throughout the Song.

"THIS THY STATURE IS LIKE TO A PALM TREE,..."
(SONG 7:7,KJV)

The palm tree is a special tree in the Bible. In Psalms 92:12, it is associated with righteousness.

> "The righteous shall flourish like the palm tree: he shall grow like a cedar in Lebanon." (KJV)

Palm trees flourish in deserts and coasts. Hurricane winds can blow against them, but they prevail. Water can become scarce, but they survive. Sand for soil might not provide enough nourishment for other trees, but the palm tree finds nutriment. Its fruit is famous for vitamins and taste. Its appearance is welcome as an oasis of refreshment from debilitating heat. Plant the righteous anywhere; they will grow, prosper, bear fruit, and be a haven of blessing for those who seek them.

Later that same Psalm speaks of the Lord being upright and then says: "there is no unrighteousness in Him (Psalms 92:15)." What He finds in the Bride is the character of a righteous person. That is His character as well. In Revelation 7:9, a multitude from every nation, tribe, and tongue assemble before the throne with palm branches in their hands. This multitude declares God gave them salvation, and the Lamb gave them deliverance. The Lamb gave them deliverance from the Law and the flesh. This deliverance is the key to the Song. No other Old Testament book alludes to such a freedom from the Law as the Song. Understanding the Song is predicated on that fact. Why are these multitudes carrying palm branches? Are these branches to symbolize what took place at Jerusalem? No, they are to symbolize the holder possesses righteousness like the palm tree.

The Bride's comparison to a palm tree in stature means she is straight and tall. Her spiritual stature is straight, and she, through righteousness, is head and shoulders above the world. Spiritually she is the destination of all who are weary in the desert. She is the oasis of love.

Palms are associated with worship in the Temple. Depicted in the temple are palm trees used as capitals for columns and intermingled with cherubim. True worship takes place within the temple of the Bride's heart. She is the exemplum of the ministry Jesus had with the Samaritan woman. True worship is within her. So full of righteousness is this Bride of Jesus, He reaches to hold her in His arms.

"I will go up to the palm tree, I will take hold of the boughs thereof": (Song 7:8 KJV)

"...THY BREASTS SHALL BE AS CLUSTERS OF THE VINE,..." (SONG 7:8,KJV)

The Bride's breasts are again defined but not as two roes. They are like clusters *of grapes*. Listen to the Lord speaking in Isaiah 65:8:

> "Thus saith the Lord, As the new wine is found in the cluster, and one saith, Destroy it not; for a blessing is in it: so will I do for my servants' sakes, that I may not destroy them all." (KJV)

Not putting new wine in old wine skins was the analogy Jesus used as the reason to establish the New Covenant. The Bride has the source of new wine within her. Her breasts are the clusters of which the Lord says is the source. This new wine is not stored in old vessels but within the body of the Bride. Look at any passage in the New Testament, and if it refers to wine, you can find its source in the Bride. The vine and branches' illustration Jesus used to reveal the closely knit relationship between Jesus and bearing of fruit is case in point. Her source of life in found in Him and being close to Him. His source of new wine is in her. These illustrations are enigmatic to what is said in the Song. The new wine of the wedding feast, the wine of the New Covenant in His blood, and the true communion of the Lord's supper are all present in this analogy.

Two great passages exist about the cluster of the vine. The first is in Song 7:8 which is followed by Jesus drawing His Bride to Him and taking the fruit of her righteousness in His hand. The second is Revelation 14:19, when the angel of the Lord thrusts into the "clusters of the earth" and casts them into the wine press of the wrath of God. The first is pressed to His bosom. The second is pressed in the wine press of the wrath of God.

"...I WILL TAKE HOLD..." (SONG 7:8,KJV)

Speaking to Himself, as if expressing that the time is right, the King declares: "I will go up...I will take hold." Going up to His Bride, He clasps the Bride in His arms. Holding righteousness to His bosom and pressing her fruit-filled life close to Him, is an intense move. Emotions are running high. Soon we will hear her response in verse 10, a rapturous response filled with satisfaction. Now, however, her proximity allows her breathing to be compared with the sweet smell of the apple and her mouth to sweet wine. Let us join what has been learned. The palm tree, in religious literature, has always stood for the victorious life. The cluster of grapes is emblematic of Israel, for even today the official symbol of the Jewish nation is the huge cluster on a shoulder rod being born by two men. The huge cluster was the symbol of abundance in the promised land. The Bride is not only victorious in her life, but she also is abundantly fruitful.

"...THE SMELL OF THY NOSE LIKE APPLES;"
(SONG 7:8,KJV)

"Apple" breath may be derived from speaking fit words. Only six times in scripture is this word *tappuach* used: four of these are in the Song. Joel has a passage about the palm tree, pomegranate, and apple tree withering as indicative of the loss of joy in the house of God. Proverbs says a word fitly spoken is like gold apples in a silver bowl (beautiful to behold and precious to own). Why did Solomon choose to point out the Bride's nose had the smell of apples? Yes, I am aware of the ancient use of all kinds of spices and aromatics to improve the breath and flavor the tongue. The absence of modern technology did not hinder them from making use of what was near, but is this the only message? Exuding from the believer, and exiting to perfume the nearest soul, is the result of speaking and virtually breathing the Word of God. Speaking fit words to a dying world characterizes the believer. Believers' mouths speak the word born of the new wine.

"...THE ROOF OF THY MOUTH LIKE THE BEST WINE..."
(SONG 7:9,KJV)

That the disciples were accused of being drunk on new wine evidenced their being filled to overflowing with the Spirit on the day of Pentecost. The mouth of the Bride is similarly judged. The "best wine" saved unto the last is cryptic of Jesus' first miracle. Not her lips, but the roof of her mouth is adjudged to have the deep drought of the new wine. She has not sipped; she has drunk freely and deeply! She is overflowing with the new wine that comes from an "upper room" life style. Jesus draws her to himself and finds her words are words of faith, and she is full of the Spirit! Is it any wonder she has fruit in abundance in her life and she stands victorious?

FROM BANNERS OVER ME, TO DESIRE FOR ME

Verse 10 hears the Bride say, "I am my beloved's and His desire is toward me." Having first declared in the banquet hall "his banner over me is love (2:4)," and then moving to "my beloved is mine and I am his (2:16)," indicates a giant step for the Bride. This declaration comes from the lips of one being kissed by her lover. She reaffirms she is totally His. She adds to the newly acquired confidence born from the stream of His love these words: "His desire is toward me." To know Jesus is "held in the galleries, (7:3)" and He desires you, is without parallel in the Word.

Three times in the scriptures the word that is used in this verse appears: twice in Genesis and once in the Song. In the two Genesis passages, "desire" is used with "ruling over" another. In the Song passage, there is no hint of "being ruled." In Genesis, the Lord said to Eve her "desire" would be toward Adam, and he would rule over her. (This is the most frequently missed part of the question: "what was Eve's curse?") In another place, God was speaking to a disturbed Cain and gives Him an alternative Cain did not take. If Cain had obeyed God, (order would have followed) then Abel's desire would have been toward Cain, and Cain would have ruled over him.

The word "desire" can be translated as "longing." In Song 7:10, I believe this is the true rendering. The Bride may be saying, "I belong to Him, and His longing is toward me." What a tribute to know your lover longs to be in your presence, longs to have you near, longs to be separated from you no more. Is this not the longing of Jesus for His Bride? This is different from the "love sick girl" declaring banners of love are flying over her. This is even different from the more learned woman who acknowledges they both have claim to each other. What we have here is a solid statement about the unity of the two being based not on the "redemption-appreciation" of the Bride, but the "redemptive-fruition" of the King. Like the whole earth groaning for the day of completion, He desires the Father to say, "This is the day." He is as eager to have the Bride (us) in His bosom, as the Bride is eager to be there.

Note what is said. The vast majority of the "church" does not have the faintest concept of this theme. Prepared virgins with trimmed lamps and full containers will understand. There is comfort to any wife when she knows her husband is so desirous of her no other will ever come between them. Paul said it in his Romans' passage: "nothing shall separate from the love of God in Christ Jesus." We, who are appreciative of redemption and cannot wait to "thank Him," are as eclipsed as the Prodigal and his waiting Father. Embraces outdo speeches. Our lives, filled with the Spirit, walking in faith and victory, already have spoken more than any words of thanksgiving. To do His will is better than the sacrifice of praise, but praise we will give.

"COME...LET US GO FORTH INTO THE FIELD;..."
(SONG 7:11,KJV)

"Us," how sweet that word sounds to a new Bride's ear. It comes on the wings of another invitation from the Bridegroom's lips. This invitation is little different in intent than the first invitation issued at the banquet hall; it is different in one aspect – she goes. "Let us go forth into the field" could well have been spoken to the disciples as easily as the Bride. They were part of the Bride. "Lo, I am with you even to the end of the earth" is the same as "let us go forth" for both goings are assured His presence.

Examine the purpose of the Bridegroom's invitation. They are to travel together and experience both field and village. They will inspect the fruit bearing vineyards and pomegranates. During their journey, he says, "I will give thee my loves." At the end of the journey, they will enter into "our gates" and dwell in the midst of all kinds of "pleasant fruits, new and old, which I have laid up for thee, O my beloved."

This journey will begin in the fields (or level places). I am reminded of Isaiah 40:3ff:

> "The voice of him that crieth in the wilderness, Prepare ye the way of the Lord, make straight in the desert a highway for our God. Every valley shall be exalted, and every mountain and hill be made low: and the crooked shall be made straight, and the rough places plain: And the glory of the Lord shall be revealed, and all flesh shall see it

together: for the mouth of the Lord hath spoken it." (KJV)

Notice the ensuing verses (Isaiah 40:6) refer to flesh being like grass and all their goodness as the flower of the field. I believe this is the same "field" as is referred to in Song 7:11. The people are the grass of that field. The Shulamite and the King are going to where the people are. The people are perishing and need their help. The grass (people) is withering and fading away. There is an antidote to death, and they possess it. The antidote is His blood. They are going to bring the good news to the people that the Blood cleanses. They are going to bring to the people the message of Luke 4, about His special anointing. They are going to bring to the people the true promises of God found in the Word. Their blessed feet together will bring life giving words to the people. They will have a ministry!

"...LET US LODGE IN THE VILLAGES. (SONG 7:11,KJV)"

The King and the Shulamite shall lodge in the villages (the little hamlets) where the people live. In their very first acts of togetherness, they launch into a ministry to the multitudes. They go where the people are. Their ministry is to review the "plantings of the Lord" and inspect their fruit. When they see "if the vine flourish, and whether or not the tender grapes appear, and if the pomegranates bud forth" they are looking for signs of life. They want to know if the branches are producing. Their interest is in life. Whatever it takes on their part to produce life, they are there to do it. Please note, while they are in the process, He will give Her His love*s*.

"...THERE WILL I GIVE THEE MY LOVES."
(SONG 7:12,KJV)

When Solomon uses the word "loves" (*dod*), it stands as a signal. Because the English language has only one word for love, we must use modifiers to mean kind, intent, and intensity of the word. Other languages have multiple words which are translated into the one form: love. In this case, *dod* is used rather than another form. *Dod* relates to the office of love and is a sexual term. In fact, *dod* is used most often in the Song. Only three other places can it be found: Proverbs 7:18 (when used as a prohibition to adultery and prostitution) and Ezekiel 16 and 23. Ezekiel chapter 23 is again a usage regarding adultery, this time in the spiritual sense. Only in Ezekiel 16:8 do we see a relationship to the Song.

> "Now when I passed by thee, and looked upon thee, behold, thy time was the time of love; and I spread my skirt over thee, and covered thy nakedness: yea, I sware unto thee, and entered into a <u>covenant</u> with thee, saith the Lord God, <u>and thou becamest mine</u>." (KJV)

What a beautiful passage this is. Covenant is more than a consummation ceremony. Covenant forms the parameter for giving and receiving His office of love. In Song 7:12, the form is plural: loves. Yes, His love is more than just salvation; it encompasses the whole range of His grace. It is holiness as well as sanctification. It is "joy unspeakable and full of glory." It is the "gifts of the Spirit." It is health and life and peace. He GIVES this as we walk with Him. Somehow, these things come to us while we minister. Somehow, the transfer takes place somewhere between our public ministry and being in His arms at night. These are special gifts given in little boxes of light at the softest moments of love. Somehow, He places in our hand a talisman, just after a kiss, and our eyes look into His eyes, filled with love and gratitude for our taking the gift. Just as our hands rest from laying them on the sick and needy, He grasps them and places a ring on our finger, just to say, "I love you." Somehow, as the day fades into darkness, we feel His arm about us and suddenly a necklace of jewels is fastened. We are His Bride!

I firmly believe all this takes place while ministering to people, for Jesus and His ministry are one. The King and the Shulamite solidify their vows among the people. If imagination has a place, imagine them meeting a blind man and Jesus saying to her, "Go ahead and lay your hands on him; he will be restored." Her reaction might well be, "But my hands are not your hands, my beloved." "Remember, we are one," comes the reply. She lifts her hands and says, "By the power of my Beloved Jesus, your eyesight is restored." The blind man leaps and shouts and praises God, for he can see. If imagination has a place, it might well be an instrument to view this couple in the villages ministering to those who are demon possessed and seeing the demons cast out. They minister together and that "togetherness" is both public and private. We next view them heading to a place all their own and a dwelling filled with surprises of His love for her. If chapter two had its banquet hall, certainly chapter seven has its treasure house.

"THE MANDRAKES GIVE A SMELL, AND AT OUR GATES ARE ALL MANNER OF PLEASANT FRUITS, NEW AND OLD, WHICH I HAVE LAID UP FOR THEE, O MY BELOVED." (SONG 7:13,KJV)

Again, if imagination has a place, it might take us to a house with gates where mandrakes give their smell, and all manners of fruits are found. It might ferry us into the solace of their dwelling where the Bride discovers things, "new and old," which have been "laid up" for her because the Bridegroom has been making provision all along for her arrival. How marvelous to know His provision is without equal and new discoveries of it are found every day. These treasures are personal and individual. There is a precedence for such activity, for Revelation sees Jesus personalizing gifts to the "angels of the churches." As He reviews their individual situations, He encourages them and promises treasures from His treasure house. Many treasures are mentioned: to eat from the tree of life, a crown of life, hidden manna, a white stone talisman with a new name written upon it, power over the nations, the morning star, white raiment, not being blotted out of the book of life (is it possible to be blotted out?), confession of his name before His Father and the angels, being made a pillar in the temple of His God, having the name of God written upon him along with the name of the city of God and Jesus' new name. These are rewards; they are gifts from the treasure house, and they are His to give. He is a giver. If He gave to "angels of the churches," why should we be surprised in His giving to His Bride? Jesus is a lover who admires, appreciates, and adorns His Bride.

Treasure houses were not strange places to Solomon. Think of the one he took the Queen of Sheba into. The Bible says she reviewed all He had. She knew about His great wealth and wisdom but would not believe it until she beheld it with her own eyes. In I Kings 10:7, we read:

> "Howbeit I believed not the words until I came, and mine eyes had seen it: and, behold, the half was not told me: thy wisdom and prosperity exceedeth the fame which I heard." (KJV)

After this account, the Bible says the Queen gave a vast amount of wealth into the King's treasury. After receiving her gifts, Solomon does a strange thing: He gives her anything she asks for. I Kings 10:13 says:

> "And king Solomon gave unto the queen of Sheba all her desire, whatsoever she asked, beside that which Solomon gave her of his ROYAL BOUNTY. So she turned and went to her own country, she and her servants."

Now I ask you, did Solomon know about giving out of the treasury house or not? Knowing what He knew about giving, isn't it reasonable to assume He included the treasure house scene in the Song for a good purpose? Through Solomon, the Spirit wished to show Jesus has greater gifts in His treasury. He wanted to show the Bride had greater privilege than a distant queen. He wanted the believer to grasp the huge difference between the treasury of heaven and the amassing of earthly possessions. If Solomon, under the blessing of heaven, could amass such a fortune, think of Jesus! If the queen of Sheba could ask what she wanted and immediately receive it from an earthly king, how much more could the Bride receive from One in love with her? The only reason the Bride of Jesus would have not is because she asked not. He wanted the believers to know, whatever they asked, they would receive. He also uses the treasure house to show more than a queen of Sheba occupies it. A Lover of Jesus is going to be treated with greater generosity than a mortal queen. Here the gifts are intimate and personal. Here they are filled with purpose and meaning. This is the place where Jesus is extremely intimate in His gift giving. No two believers will come away with identical treasures. Revelation and rhema to us are unique and individual, and we find them both in His treasure house!

He is constantly bestowing gifts from the treasure house. As long as He sees us receiving them, using them, and rejoicing in them, He will keep pouring them on. How it makes His heart joyful to see us examine, then appropriate, then wear, each grace gift He gives. The gifts in revelation are not just spiritual gifts; He maintains balance between the material and the spiritual. All the gifts He gives to us will not be spiritual. He wants us to know He gives material gifts as well. His gifts, both material and spiritual, must be received in the intimacy of the giving. Just as prayer reaches into the place of extreme intimacy with Jesus, so His revelations are found to be wrapped in that same covering. Treasures new and old are not the same for every believer; neither are they universal in identity, but rather they are hand picked for the person receiving them. The Bride is unique, and her gifts are specially chosen. Solomon understood well this principle and with deftness included each element in the Song when he wrote: "There is treasure to be desired and oil in the dwelling of the wise...(Prov 21:20)."

From this scripture, I wish to add a note about the Bride preparing gifts for her Jesus. It would be ludicrous to conceive of a treasure house only filled with treasure from His store. The Proverbs passage declares treasure and oil is in the house of those who are wise. We are told in James to ask wisdom, and we would have it given to us. Along with wisdom comes the blessings of it, both spiritual and material. When we lay up treasures in heaven, we lay up our gifts to Him, our treasures to be dealt to Him, our love gifts especially modeled and wrapped for Him. Let history record out of the good treasure of our hearts flows the currency of heaven. I have a treasure house in which my offerings to Him are recorded and kept; I can withdraw love gifts and use them in heaven or on earth. I can send them around the world and bestow them in Jesus' Name. I can lavish on this earth and its people mighty portions of favor and grace which have been received and stored. They are mine to give; He gave them to me. In the night season, when lying upon my bed and in His presence, I can give to Him from my treasure and find He receives and is glad.

What is your relationship to Him if it is not as the Bride?

CHAPTER ELEVEN

THE SEALED HEART

"Set me as a seal upon thine heart, as a seal upon thine arm"
(Song 8:6 KJV)

UNDERSTANDING

In the Song, often the dialogue itself produces understanding. Why the translators break between chapters 7 and 8 at this time, I cannot tell. If you read past the chapter heading, you will realize the Bride's response is a continuation of their love dialogue. She is exploring those things new and old which are hers to possess. What are these items new and old? In His infinite wisdom, the Bridegroom knew they would arrive at the treasure house at the correct moment. How short or long is the distance to the treasure house from the banquet room? The distance depends on the individual believer often times. Some seem to arrive in a flash, and others get there only after years of struggle. Be assured of one thing – they must all arrive. John 17 has part of its answer to Jesus' prayer in the treasure house. In John 17:22 and 26, we find key verses related to this house:

> "And the glory which thou gavest me I have given them; that they may be one, even as we are one:...that the love wherewith thou hast loved me may be in them, and I in them." (KJV)

In these verses Jesus is praying for His own, and He is giving to them the treasures He received from His Father. In verse 24, Jesus wills for every believer to be with Him, which in itself is a great treasure. Do you remember Jesus said to His disciples they were to lay up for themselves treasures in heaven where the corrupting and thieving elements could not touch them? Are these treasures to be selfishly maintained for our own use or are they to be given others in an abundance that matches His? Are these treasures, in the heavenly treasure house, not repositories for love gifts we wish to bestow on Him? I know they are! To receive His gift is one thing, but to give Him one of our gifts is another. Here is where intimate giving takes place. Yes, I know our gifts may not parallel His. Sometimes it may seem we are like children making crayon drawings of hearts to give to a parent, but observe how precious are those drawings.

If you can imagine the interplay in that treasure room as the Bridegroom gives and the Bride receives, you can understand the great bonding that is also taking place. They are one. The culmination of bonding requires the treasure house. There _is_ similarity between the banquet house and the treasure house.

Just how are these two houses similar? The banquet hall changes the Bride's life, for it acts as an arena for her spiritual expansion. She first sees the magnitude of the Bridegroom's kingdom, its vast spiritual import, and its immeasurable supply while she is in the banquet house. In the treasure house, she glimpses, with mature faith, the scope of His provision. While in the treasure house, she also fathoms how important it is for Him to give gifts. These gifts have taken time to accumulate. When Jesus said He was going to heaven to prepare a place for us, He was including vast provision in that preparation. Jesus is a giver; He delights in providing for His Beloved. His eyes are alive with tenderness when He gives her those especially prepared gifts. From Genesis' earliest light to the very present hour, He has garnered treasures for her. His quest for treasure trove is boundless. Even into the future, He reaches to excess to adorn His Bride. Graces unimaginable await her hand to receive them. Whatever she might deem to be a lack is more than supplied for her taking. As jewelry comes alive when worn on the flesh and person of the wearer, so grace comes alive when adorning the believer.

Many treasures, both material and spiritual, await the touch of the believer. Once aware of their presence, once aware of the reality they can be possessed now, we often stand awestruck and immobile. Our desire is increased by the fact we now know we must stretch our faith to receive them, to reach for that which previously has been unheard of, and walk in realms beyond our past comprehension. Treasures have been there a long time waiting for us to arrive at the place we can receive them. Thus, we resemble the Shulamite and are eager to receive, but because we are flesh, we still measure our life based on our ability and capacity. His treasure trove corresponds to grace and must be received by faith. His gifts are not measured by our current capacity but the capacity we will achieve when He adds His grace. These are grace gifts, and because they are, they must be received as grace is received. (An example: Intercessory Prayer is a grace gift through the Holy Spirit which must be received by faith in the same manner as salvation. The moment we appropriate that grace gift by faith and receive it in faith, then at that moment, we possess it, and we begin to operate in its power. It is His will all the treasures, new and old, be ours, but they are to be received in faith.

"O THAT THOU WERT AS MY BROTHER,..."
(SONG 8:1, KJV)

The Shulamite, in receiving her treasures from Him and enjoying His giving to her, virtually bursts into chapter eight verse one:

> "O that thou wert as my brother, that sucked the breasts of my mother! When I should find thee without, I would kiss thee; yea, I should not be despised." (Song 8:1 KJV)

Strange passage isn't it, but not so strange when viewed from the point of social and cultural acceptability. The desire to kiss the King in public, even outside the treasure room, would be less censored if He had been the Shulamite's brother. Her elation is evident, but why is she so concerned about decorum? This Bride is flesh, and what she experiences is on earth. She knows what it means to be despised. Her connection to Jesus brings to her the same responses the world affords Him. He was despised; she is despised. The more the Bride invests herself in Jesus, the more intense will be the world's reaction. This world, its churches, its religions, its customs, its society does not receive the true Bride with open arms. These reactions have little to do with the end time tribulation but are the actions of jealousy by a religious world unwilling to come first to the banquet hall and then to the treasure house! Just as Jesus was despised and rejected by His own people (the deeply religious community of His day), so the Bride will feel rejection from her own religious community. It was not a group of infidels who crucified Him; it was a group of the sanctioned.

Might there be another element involved in this passage? Yes, there is the reconciliation between Jesus being the Bride's spiritual brother and at the same time her husband. If brother, one set of rules applies; if husband, another. We see this born out in the subsequent passage when she contemplates bringing him into the house of her mother for instruction. Customarily, a girl went to her mother for instruction prior to marriage. (For instance, one mother so instructed her daughter, "Worship and adore him, and he shall be your slave forever, but if you act churlishly toward him, you will be his servant forever.") Even men went to their mothers for marriage instruction; a good example is in Proverbs 31, when a mother tells what qualities to look for in a woman.

The Shulamite clearly has a problem, and the problem is how to present her love for the Bridegroom to a world hostile to Him. Her dilemma causes the Shulamite to seek flesh answers to spiritual problems. (Abraham did the same thing when he told Sarah to declare herself to be his sister rather than his wife.) Where will the Shulamite then find her answer? Her answer, like ours, is not found in behavioral patterns but is found in His arms. No, the law of love has superseded the law of rules, and she must grasp this truth. Social formulas and religious decorum, along with accepted practices of the church and the world, must be discarded. She must show her love without respect to the world around her.

The Bride's kisses are acceptable to the Bridegroom anytime. Her embraces are welcomed by Him in public view or in sweet solitude. Gratitude, expressed in private or in public, is never inappropriate. "Inappropriate" must become a lost word in her vocabulary. When the Spirit moves in her heart, she must do what He says, whether deemed appropriate by her or not.

Again, explore the matter of brother versus husband. In Genesis, technically the first Adam (who was created in the image of God from the "dust of the earth") was a brother to Eve. She was created by the same father out of him and bore part and particle of his being in her body. She was also his bride. Should it be different in the second Adam who is "the Lord from heaven"? Spiritually, He is brother to the Bride as well as husband. She is part and particle of His very being. She came out of Him. The Bride of Jesus has His blood, His person, His being on the inside of her. Grace has changed her from a "world-being" to a "heaven-being." She is His "sister-Bride."

"...I WOULD CAUSE THEE TO DRINK OF SPICED (MIXED) WINE..." (SONG 8:2, KJV)

In her unique position, can she find instruction from her mother? No! Even if we consider Mother Israel to be her spiritual progenitor, she cannot return to the Law for instruction. Neither can communion be based on mixed wine and old order traditions. Chapter 8 verse 2 ends all discussion, all consideration, and all reference to anything related to the world, its church, or its custom. Mixed wine is continually being offered on the altars of this world, and it will not satisfy. Yet, this is a peculiar wine, for it is made from the juice of the pomegranate.

Spiritual fertility (pomegranate) is not based on the blend of social and religious custom. (Wouldn't you know it; mixed wine from pomegranates is mentioned only once in all the scripture. The only time in the Bible the word spiced *reqach* (compounded, mixture, spiced) is used in this connection is in this one verse. Solomon is pointing out the spiritual truth that a mixture offered by the Bride is unacceptable. The greatest test the church will have in the last days concerns this mixture. Let me go on record at this point and say openly the sacred and the profane is an unacceptable mixture, and it must not be offered to Jesus. The Bride virtually says in these verses, "If you were my brother, things would be easy. If you were an ordinary bridegroom, I could find instruction from the customary sources. If I were the ordinary bride, I could bring to you a mixture of that which has been taught me, and that which I personally possess, and you would find it acceptable. If I were an ordinary bride...." She isn't.

Sociologically speaking, every couple brings to their wedding a blend of all they have experienced, been taught, and assimilated culturally. Persons bring to the marriage their individual hopes, dreams, fantasies, and, sadly, their hang ups and neuroses. Each expects the other to drink deeply the mixture he or she offers. This may work for ordinary couples, although it is the cause of conflict, but not in this union. Solomon (Jesus) and the Shulamite (Bride) are not ordinary. Ordinary stuff doesn't work here!

"...HIS RIGHT HAND SHOULD EMBRACE ME."
(SONG 8:3,KJV)

The embrace these two engage in is not ordinary either. In verse three, we find the couple embracing in similar manner as they embraced in the banquet hall. Some translators make this a fantasy of the Bride by emphasizing the "should" in each line. She is doing some wistful thinking in their estimation. Solomon, however, may have used "should" to signal the differences and similarities of the two situations. After the banquet hall embrace, she does not accompany him, but journeys into her own will. After the treasure house embrace, she is never separated from Him. The two embraces take place under similar circumstances, as both occasions follow a revelation of His vast provision. Both occasions find Him initiating the embrace. Both occasions elicit a charge to the daughters of Jerusalem not to awaken love until HE pleases.

"WHO IS THIS THAT COMETH UP FROM THE WILDERNESS,..." (SONG 8:5,KJV)

The daughters of Jerusalem pose a question similar to the one posed in Chapter 3 verse 6. "Who is this that cometh up from the wilderness?" They have an "add-on" to their question in this verse though, and it is, "leaning upon her beloved." In the former, the Bridegroom alone is coming from His instruction in the presence of God. Now both he and the Bride are coming forth from that instruction, and she is leaning on HIM. When Jesus and His Bride are receiving in the same way, at the same time, and from the same source, they are one. Just as the Lord Jesus received from the Father all He spoke and did, in like manner, the Shulamite receives.

This prophecy is coming to a rapid close, so its author is settling some basic issues. Close to the time of their wedding, the Bride's and Bridegroom's lives are being concertized from heaven. They act in complete unity and oneness. Their lives are so blended their concerns are identical. The verses which follow are repeated statements of solidarity and complementarity. (Note: I use the word complement which, in reality, is the sum of the epistle of John. The Epistle speaks overtly about a communion which supersedes all other concepts of love and lends itself to total fulfillment.) Was not the first Adam's need met by the first Eve? Is not the second Adam's need met in the second Eve? As devastating as this concept is to traditional religious thought, it is nonetheless biblically born out.

The sole reason for the existence of the Bride is to be the spiritual companion of the Groom. She was born for this reason, nurtured for this reason, yea, lives for this purpose. The daughters say it this way:

> "I raised thee up under the apple tree: there thy mother brought thee forth: there she brought thee forth that bare thee." (Song 8:5 KJV)

"SET ME AS A SEAL UPON THINE HEART,..."
(SONG 8:6,KJV)

Perhaps the greatest appeal to the believer today is issued in the passage found in Song 8:6:

> "Set me as a seal upon thine heart, as a seal upon thine arm:" (KJV)

The Bible clearly says the Holy Spirit seals us to redemption. Didn't the Romans and the Jews seek to seal Jesus in a tomb, and didn't that seal break so the Greater One could set His seal? Why is it necessary to be set as a seal on the heart? Revelation has an answer again. Revelations' Seals, each broken to reveal another move of God in History, indicate the power of a seal. Didn't the King's signet, set in wax and unbroken, offer a guarantee of validity to the recesses of the sealed envelope? Isn't this similar to what takes place in our lives? Jesus breaks the seal of death so He can place a greater seal of Love on our hearts. His seal on our heart is our assurance God is moving in our history and our hearts will be delivered intact unto the day of redemption. Is not the King's seal on us, so the world cannot break it, so no tribulation or trial can cause the ruin of the contents of our being? The gates into our hearts must be sealed away from this world and to be opened only by Him. Somehow, we must set that seal on our heart through faith; somehow, it must occupy our will; somehow, it must remain as a reminder of whose we are.

"Set _Me_ as the seal upon thine heart," the Scripture says. Is Jesus the seal on our hearts? Is His person the first consideration of all we ask or think? "Set _Me_," as opposed to the seal of any other, is His cry. "Set Me" is the appeal of one who wants to be our first consideration and our last. It is the plea of One who loves us so much He longs to occupy that area of our life where decisions are made and from whence the issues of life go forth. "Set Me, and I will be the responsible one, I will be the protector, I will be the guarantor," is His plea. Because the appeal is for a seal to be set on the heart and the arm, we know its purpose is more than a phylactery.

Jews set phylacteries on their head and arm as outward signs of their devotion to the Holy Scriptures. They displayed these bindings without shame and as proudly as they bore their fleshly circumcision. To the non-Jewish world, these phylacteries were a symbol of the Jews' difference as a people and their special service to their God. To the Jewish world, they were constant reminders they were people of difference, people responsive to the commandments of their God. No Jew could enter into carnal intercourse without having to deal with his difference. He was circumcised. Instantly, his circumcision set him apart from the rest of the ancient world. The outward cutting of the flesh failed to produce an inward circumcision, however. In like manner, phylacteries failed to produce an inward change. Circumcision failed to produce fidelity and faithfulness. It was supposed to be an outward seal on the body as a testimony of a more real covenant within. Outward displays fail. Seals on the heart never fail to produce their desired result. Worn inwardly on the heart, and manifesting itself outwardly on the arm and the head, this seal serves to tell a world "we are different, we belong to someone whom to us is higher than all earthly considerations of power and intellect!" Our seal is a person. Our seal is Jesus. Worn on our heart, He protects His garden. Worn on our arm (sign of our will) and about the mind, He protects our flesh and mind until we join Him at the wedding.

> "Nevertheless the foundation of God standeth sure, having this seal, The Lord knoweth them that are his." (II Tim 3:19 KJV)

"...FOR LOVE IS STRONG AS DEATH, JEALOUSY IS CRUEL AS THE GRAVE....IF A MAN WOULD GIVE ALL THE SUBSTANCE OF HIS HOUSE...IT WOULD UTTERLY BE CONTEMNED." [WOULD HE BE CONDEMNED?]
(SONG 8:6-7, KJV)

It is Jesus' sworn love that conquers the strength of death. Such love has as strong a claim on the believer's life as death has on the flesh. This love rivals the power of death and is stronger than its grip. When death would close on our mortal flesh and make its Adamic claim, at that very moment, His love will flood our being and whisper to His Bride, "You will have nothing to fear as you walk through this valley." It is His jealousy over us that overcomes the grave and the vehement flames of Hell. It is His love that raises a "standard against the flood."

Often our love for Jesus rises up in us in the form of jealousy. When we see things that hurt His church, and wound His loved ones, jealousy rises within us. We are jealous for Him. When we view the disparaging clamor of so-called "divine worship," we are jealous for Him. This love we possess is not purchased love, although Calvary cost Him; it is voluntary love.

The Song makes an interesting statement at this point, "If a man would give all the substance of his house for love, it would utterly be contemned." Is the Bride or the Bridegroom to be condemned for such consuming love? The man who is "contemned" is the one who gives all his worldly possessions seeking to buy love. This Jesus purchased salvation out of a loving heart but He did not purchase love. We are "bought with a price," meaning our redemption is paid for, but we must receive Him out of a loving heart as an act of love. In Jesus' house of love, substance abounds; and together He and the Bride share the riches of His inheritance, for they are sealed as one!

CONCERN FOR OTHERS

"We have a little sister, and she hath no breasts: what shall we do for our sister in the day when she shall be spoken for?" (Song 8:8 KJV)

One of the very first matters in the heart of the sealed believer concerns those like her but who have not yet reached maturity. Such outreach is normal and is the concern of all who truly regard Jesus as their own. The reason is not just to "share" Him, as so many church groups are willing to do, but to introduce another to the depth of devotion we possess. No greater exploit could be entered on by humankind. I call it an exploit for two reasons: first, the scripture says we shall do exploits; second, the purpose of our doing is to gather those who are His and snatch them away from the evil one. Reaching into the life of another takes Divine power and strategy.

Not a single soul is born into the kingdom, and deeply in love with Jesus, without these elements. Somewhere someone has to claim that person through determination and intercession. Allowing oneself to be used of the Holy Spirit, many times a strategy beyond the scope of a person's thinking is set on, and he or she follows it. Many are they who have been led by the Spirit to do bizarre and strange things (relative to their own thinking), only to find themselves in the path of the very one for whom they longed. It is at this juncture we learn to be responsive in prayer and positioning to the leadership of the inward Spirit.

"IF SHE BE A WALL,..." (SONG 8:9, KJV)

"If she be a wall" is the same testimony given by the Bride in verse 10. "I am a wall" is her exclamation. Listen to the strategy the Bride is going to use. "If this virgin is like me, we will build on her (character)," is a paraphrase of the Bride's strategy. She further declares the edifice to be built on her character is "a palace of silver." What does it mean to build a "palace of silver" on a person? Remember this person is a wall, which means she is a wall of resistance to the world. Remember this person is eligible (for future brideship) but has not matured to a place where she can make a commitment. Her life must be built up. Remember, this person has the same qualities as the Shulamite. On these foundations, a marvelous palace of great price can be built. Still, there is another consideration to be made; if the young virgin is not a wall, then what?

"...IF SHE BE A DOOR,..." (SONG 8:9, KJV)

"If she be a door," (and thus open to every wind of doctrine) "we will inclose her with boards of cedar." Doors are like that; they may open to every idea and concept that comes along. Doors are made to open in response to a knock or to close out an unwelcome intruder. This is why in Revelation Jesus says He: "stands at the door and knocks." (In South America it is customary to build a wall of protection around a site before beginning construction. This wall is to protect what is inside and to give entrance only to trusted workers. So it is with those who are not yet matured; often it is necessary to house them about until they are complete within.) "Walls of cedar" denote wood that is impenetrable by destructive elements and insects. Its sweet smell is pungently acceptable to those in its presence and signals the smell of death to those who would seek to destroy it.

PERSONAL TESTIMONY: "I AM A WALL,... AND I AM FAVORED..." (SONG 8:10, KJV)

Having reached a place of spiritual maturity, the Bride declares she is a citadel against all that is anti-Christ. She is a wall. Any word, any thought, any message contrary to the anointing on her is immediately rejected. She is full grown. She is a spiritual wall of resistance and protection for the garden of her heart. She has "breasts like towers" which reveal maturity and plenty. She is succor to those who come to her. She is as watchful and cautious as one who builds a tower in a vineyard to keep away the intruder and interloper.

Notice, this is the Bride's testimony! She is using the Bridegroom's terms. Her testimony uses "I am" and "my" in the same commanding way He has used them formally. She is delivering her soul in concise measure to His measure. She is His complement; she is His equal in strength, desire, concern, and adornment. The anointing on Him now rests on her. Imputed as it may be, she reigns with Him. Just as He imputes righteousness to us who are not righteous in our own right, in that same manner, she is imputed Queenship (the ability to reign). We act as righteous because He said we could. She acts as Queen because He said she could!

"...THEN WAS I IN HIS EYES AS ONE WHO FOUND FAVOR." (SONG 8:10,KJV)

"Then was I," begins the next part of the Bride's ongoing witness. "Then" is such a word of interruption, for it is used to alert the reader of a change. Whether the occasion be terrible or grand, that one word inoculates the situation. The Bride uses the word as a culminating word. It is a word of moment and carries the weight of intensity. "Then was I" at this moment, having witnessed the culmination of all the events of my history, "as one who found favor." After all of her growing, maturing, experiencing, faithing, she testifies: "In His eyes I was as one that found favour." In this verse, the word "favor" in hebrew is *shalom*. It means peace, prosperity, and completeness. In whose eyes were these found? In Jesus' eyes! In His eyes, she is found possessing peace, prosperity, and completeness. (It makes me want to jump up and shout!)

All through the Old Testament, there are occasions cited where someone found favor. These passages use a different Hebrew word, *chen*, which also means favor. Most of the passages utilize this basic word. Ruth found favor with Boaz. Esther found favor with the King. Jesus found favor with God and man. (I am acquainted with this kind of favor in my life as a believer. I have given favor and received such from many hands. As a teacher, it is an everyday occurrence. To the student who is desirous of learning, I seek to open paths. It is my desire to assist or help to break down barriers. I desire to encourage and help in any way possible to see him or her achieve. If a teacher who sees a willing student is able to show favor, how much more a lover like Jesus, but this is not the favor found in the Song.)

Peace, prosperity, and completeness occupy a different level of favor than the kind just mentioned. These encompass the combined favor of Ruth and Esther plus the three components of *shalom*. Because the Bride is full of grace and truth, what could she possibly lack in the wake of the Bridegroom's pledge? Although she experienced His favor manifested in so many ways previously, it was not reality to her until now. As such reality lands on the shore of our heart, it liberates!

PROSPERITIES BUSINESS:
"SOLOMON HAD A VINEYARD..." (SONG 8:11)

In order for Jesus to supply my prosperity, He must possess it. So, the action moves away from the fact He will supply our every need to an example of how that wealth has been accumulated. In verse 11, Solomon speaks of having vineyards as a business; while in verse 12, the Shulamite speaks of a vineyard as a possession. "Solomon had a vineyard at Baal-hamon," is how she begins the exemplum. Baal-hamon is symbolic. Baal-hamon has several meanings which relate directly to increase, one of which is "lord of abundance." One of the others is "lord of the now," which emphasizes abundance is for the present. Another meaning is "lord of the multitudes," which could refer to the magnitude of that abundance among the saints. It could also be interpreted "lord of the last hour," referring to our getting ready for the final harvest.

Solomon "sharecrops" with "keepers" who are to bring a portion of the abundance to Him as owner. Notice the abundance is great, for His portion is "a thousand pieces of silver." The keepers are provided for; but out of the abundance of the harvest, they give Him a perfect amount. Today, those keepers bring the firstfruits unto Jesus. Those true keepers hearken to the voice of Jesus and do His bid, even as Solomon's keepers did his. They live off the abundance of what is sown in good ground. They call Him the "Lord of Increase." They refer to Him as the God of the "now." Their abundance is not distant and heavenly; their abundance and share are in the "now." Because He is "Lord of the Multitudes," we have no clue as to the number of keepers who work for Him and the amount of abundance they possess. We know this; the Bride is satisfied she can rest in Him and feel completely at peace. He has sufficiency enough to meet any demand!

"...TO BRING A THOUSAND PIECES OF SILVER."
(SONG 8:11,KJV)

The anomaly of "pieces of silver" is very significant. The price paid to Judas was a "broken pittance in kind" to that which is paid by the keepers. I am sure Judas had no inkling as to the power of representation those coins contained. The Lord of the Harvest considers them to be like selling Judas' soul for a mess of pottage.

I believe the reference to a thousand pieces of silver means a vast amount of wealth. In the eyes of a shepherd girl it was a king's ransom. The vastness of His incoming wealth means the treasure house will never be empty.

"MY VINEYARD...IS BEFORE ME:...(SONG 8:12,KJV)"

What a statement! Looking at the Bridegroom; the Bride finds her abundance in Him. All she needs is standing before her. The supplier of every need, the bastion against all storms, the cry against every creditor stands before her. He BELONGS to her. She says it like this: "My vineyard which is mine."

That Solomon had thousands of vineyards may reflect the vastness of His resources and the streams flowing into it. By contrast, there are just a few who are charged with keeping the abundant crops and the constant flow. Could it be in reality, "Many are called, but few chosen?" Could it be within the frame work of abundance, there are just a few who find themselves partakers with Him? Our wealth is not in the vastness of Jesus' earthly provision; it is in HIM. If we say, like the Bride, "my vineyard is before me," we are calling Him more precious than any provision.

Vineyards are precious to the owners. We know Ahab's and Jezebel's covetousness of Naboth's vineyard struck them down. Naboth's vineyard represented His inheritance, and he was unwilling to part with his inheritance. Oh church, our vineyard is "Thou" (Jesus). We are unwilling to part with our inheritance. We consider our vineyard precious. He is the source of wealth and substance for all generations that follow.

Yet, the vineyard passage is a balance symbolism. I use the word balance because early in the Song, the vineyard parallel was used by the Shulamite. She lamented having to keep the vineyard of others and not being able to care for her own vineyard (self). In this verse, she again is not occupied with self but finds she is satisfied in caring for another. When she says, "My vineyard, which is mine, is before me," a balance is created in the whole story. No longer is she concerned about the care of her life; she is concerned with the care of another: His name is Jesus! Solomon's inspiration chose this moment to create balance in the text. He takes the code word "vineyard," which He introduced in Chapter One, and uses it to show the maturity of the Bride. His use of balance is also seen in the use of the Banquet Hall and the Treasure House. The two watchmen scenes, the harmonious descriptions given in sequence by the Lovers, the inclusions of multiple word choices such as myrhh, frankincense, hart, and roe are examples of literary genius.

"THOU THAT DWELLEST IN THE GARDENS,... CAUSE ME TO HEAR..." (SONG 8:13,KJV)

Who dwells in the gardens? It is easy for you to answer now, Jesus! In the many gardens of the heart, you will always find Him. You will find Him living there. Protecting, planting, working His works of grace, these are His doings. Pronouncement is also part of His work in the gardens. He who spoke worlds into being has something to say. Something worth listening to gets and keeps the attention of the hearer. Those who work with Him hearken to His voice. (There is an old southern saying: "I will not believe it until I hear it from the horse's mouth." Many an old timer has released himself from a conversation with those words. The meaning behind such a statement is powerful. It precludes opinion, gossip, hearsay, interpretation, addition, selectivity, and all sorts of misunderstanding. To hear, from the mouth of the one who spoke concerning a matter, gives credence to that which is spoken and proper interpretation to the hearer. A true friend often would utter such a phrase out of loyalty. A doubter might also use this as a ploy indicating he alone would be the judge on hearing the matter from the originator. Regardless of the reason, the Song says those who are his companions "hearken to His voice.") His voice is unique and worth dropping whatever task may have one's interest to care for what He is saying.

Who are these companions? One might conjecture Jesus is referring to His earthly companions, the disciples. To hear, as the disciples heard, would immediately bring into play all the New Testament's written Word, plus all the acts and deeds of faith they performed. It would bring to mind the faithfulness to detail of Philip, who heard and immediately acted on what he heard (ie: his going to the Ethiopian eunuch). It would encompass the Isle of Patmos and the jail of Paul. It would include "hearing in the Spirit" as well as the actual voice of the Saviour. It would mean knowing the Word as they knew it and being able to apply Old Testament pronouncements to situations as they did. It would mean "plying in the Spirit" matters of immediate concern and having the ability to ferret out, through the "spirit of discernment," those who are like Ananias and

Sapphira. It would mean being sensitive to the "move of the Spirit" which would bring one to confront the lame and the blind and know exactly what to say and do. It would mean not traveling to some places (like Paul who was prevented from entering a country). It would mean being able to "see in the Spirit" those things you were interpreting wrongly, as Peter did on the roof top of Cornelius' house. It would mean following "His voice" just to get to the roof top!

Who are these companions? If you look at the Hebrew word *chaber* and those places in scriptures where it appears in that form, such a study would reveal that only in limited circumstances does it so appear. Its meaning considers a factor not fully gleaned from a tertiary look. Meanings like companion, fellow, and "being knit together" are indicative of a closer walk than just a "believer." It carries a deepening effect "like being bound together," "coupled," " being joined together," or "having complete fellowship with someone." Blooming forth now are all the writings of the epistles of John.

> "...truly our fellowship is with the Father, and with his Son Jesus Christ." (I John 1:3 KJV)

The Spanish language has a word, *compañerismo.* This word relates to the English word communion. Being *compañero* to someone is different than being in communion with them. *Compañerismo* is associated with a feeling tone which denotes "being along side" someone. Communion is more, too, than just bread and wine; it is an "entering into" type fellowship. In the Song, we can truthfully say those who have entered into and enjoy a companionship with Jesus want to hear His voice.

Who are these companions? David says he is a companion of all who fear the Lord and keep his precepts (Ps.119:63 KJV). Ezekiel uses the word to show the joining together of the divided kingdom. He models two sticks with names written on them and joins them in his hand, thus showing their being brought together as one. When inquired of as to the meaning, he says, "This is the house of Israel in the hand of God." This is the same as covenant. Graphically displayed in His hand is the phrase of Jesus, "No man can pluck them out of my Father's hand!" Companionship with Jesus requires having our names written, being held in the Father's hand, and being joined in an everlasting covenant with Him. Candidly, I cry to every reader; this is not the picture of every church member! Falsely, the multitudes depend on that which is "sanctioned" to suffice for their salvation. As sadly as the Pharisees and Sadducees were lost from Jesus because of similar error, so vast numbers are lost now. We must adjust the universally accepted picture! His definition alone is the only one which will stand. Only those who will hear His voice say, "Enter thou into the joy of thy salvation," are the ones who will have "salvation."

When the Bride says "Cause me to hear thy voice," she is adding a quantity unspoken: "Like <u>they</u> hearken to thy voice (paraphrased)!" Here is the magnificent truth to the Bride in the closing days of this world. There are only two considerations which must be hers: hearing His voice, and calling for His return.

If ever a book challenges the modern church, it is this book! When the Bride says, "I want to hear you, to respond to you just like the closest knit of your companions," she is speaking out of a heart already conditioned. She has experienced maturity; she has viewed the Bridegroom's magnificence and felt His embrace. She is aware of His vast provision and His willingness to lavish it on her. She is cognizant of her position in time and eternity. She is standing in the full light of His Word and is at the point of reigning as His equal. She comprehends her future and is assured of her own glorification. She is rooted and grounded with a strong foundation. Her maturity has led her to be in harmony and symphony with Him. She is parallel to Paul, who cries out after all he knows and has written, "That I may be found of Him," and again, "That I may know Him and the power of His resurrection."

When the Bride says, "Cause me to hearken to thy voice," she is saying the most important item for her consideration is to hear and hearken to the Bridegroom's voice. In the first chapter of the Song, the Shulamite is invited to join the Shepherd boy's companions to feed her sheep. In the last verses of the Song, she cries, "Let me be one of those companions so knit to you, so joined to you, so in step with you, I can respond to you like they respond." In these few verses are the Bride's last words.

Last words are deemed to be the most important. Sermons have been written on the last words of Jesus on the cross as well as the last words of Jesus as He was taken into the clouds. Somehow, even our own loved one's last words hold unique significance to most of us. Well, the last words of the Bride, after she enters the ranks of "those who always hearken to His voice," are: "Make haste my beloved." The echo of those words across a thousand years saw their answer in red letters: "Surely, I come quickly (Revelation 22:20)." The Revelator heard these two lovers and their dialogue in the eternities and exclaimed like the true Bride: "Even so, come Lord Jesus." The Bride sent forth Her request more than nine hundred years before Jesus was born; and in the timelessness of His kingdom, we all heard her answer to that request in Revelation 22.

Blessed are those who see these truths! Blessed are those to whom the Spirit shall quicken their understanding in these last days. Blessed are those who see in the mirror of their heart: THE BRIDE.

> O, the mystery of the Book,
> Which Solomon claimed as his own,
> Could not be fathomed in its power,
> Until the church be fully grown,
> For cloistered in the heart,
> Of this wise and ancient King,
> Were truths so great and powerful,
> T'would make his heart to sing.
>
> More than Moses' sister's Song,
> Sweet ballad of a Miriam,
> The theme to this His "Song,"
> Choired in heaven's delirium,
> Is: "Now the 'rule of Law' is lost,
> Beneath the waves of Love!"
>
> –C.R.Oliver

ADDENDUM 1

THOUGHTS ON THE BANQUET HALL

I include these thoughts about the banquet hall, more to get them off my chest than to add some great new light. I do strongly believe that the banquet hall was designed to incorporate all that Jesus paid for at Calvary. I also believe that Solomon did not intend for the reader to confuse this with a smorgasbord where the believer could determine which dishes to choose and which to leave based on a matter of taste. He does wish for us to have "delight" (see comment on "delight" in addendum 2) and that element is a part of the banquet scene. The banquet hall is the answer to all who hunger and thirst after righteousness. When I review the banquet hall scene, there is a certain element of never being satisfied with the way I handle it. It seems that any light (tertiary) rendering of its impact and import is too surface and lacks the depth to be found there. My reasoning is twofold: first, He (Jesus) prepared it. Based on John 14 (which I consider to be one of the greatest passages in the Word), I would place great credence to His preparation. If we are depending on Him to construct our eternal residence, we are also leaving all the design and placement to Him as well. The banquet hall is also His construction, His preparation and design, and it is sufficient to meet every need of man. Like manna, it is a daily provision, and unlike a buffet, this meal is prepared with you and your spiritual needs in mind. I said my reasoning was twofold; the second is as inclusive as the first: He is the only one in this hall with the Bride. This is very significant because He has directive power and with this comes the element of teaching about fulfillment of need. Selectivity within range is a powerful tool. I often say the greatest power a minister executes is in this realm. He chooses what topics, how much depth will be used to cover the topic, and the time spent with it.

Jesus wants to be alone with His Bride in the banquet hall. Here, He selects, decides the portion, and determines the value of the meal. Daniel's prophecy includes a section at the beginning when much ado is made over the type of food chosen by the foursome. Daniel and his three companions do not eat of the King's meat. It is my belief so much emphasis was given this because it acts as a prototype of the Believer. We cannot partake, on a regular basis, that which is prepared for the general public. Their religious order and social structure cannot produce the kind of faith filled person Jesus will call His Bride.

It is from this banquet hall our spiritual meals must find their origin. So convinced am I of this a short perusal of anemic Christendom will convince anyone. Private meals with Jesus, prepared by Him and chosen for their content, are an absolute must in the Kingdom if the "fair" status is to be obtained. Such will not be based on our appraisal of our condition but His appraisal. He can look and tell if we have been "eating right."

In this banquet hall is every promise found in the Word of God. Jesus came into a world that already had proven to God; in example and history, there are universal and individual needs. Universal food is served everyday from the Word, and man needs such, but until it is individualized and served us by the Holy Spirit, our anemia will continue to show. Until what He has provided is appropriately taken into our Being and assimilated as nourishment and truth to us, it is "cast out in the draught" and has no value to us. Allow me to give an example: John 12:12,13,14. These verses, taken within context and appropriated for our nourishment, stand rotting on the plates of most of Christendom. When a believer gets alone with Jesus, takes this as nourishment, and it becomes a part of that believer's person and life structure, it produces a transformed person.

The banquet hall has other elements worth exploring. One of those elements is wine. Distillation of wine is not totally the "vine and grape" teaching of the New Testament but includes other fruits as well. As in the natural world, wine is derived from many fruit sources. The fruit of being with Jesus is a heady experience, like that which is derived from drinking wine. In verse 3 of chapter two, the Bride declares, "His fruit was sweet to my taste." Readily, one will jump to the "fruits of the spirit" and confine his or her thinking to these parameters if not careful. Tasting of Him is more than that! "You must be out of your mind (Mark 3:20,21)," has been the unwelcome conclusion incurred by many a saint on determining a course of direction derived from tasting of His fruit. Courses of action and roads to destiny have drawn much of the same response both from the religious and secular world. We eat of the Lord at the Lord's table.

One other element to catch our review is found in "who brought whom." Our need might be a factor in entering the banquet hall, but this is not the case of the Shulamite. He does the bringing. This lessens the chances of our being our own discerner as to time. A period of "shadow sitting and fruit delighting," preceded entrance. I suspect it still does. It's His call all the way in the realm of the Spirit.

Somehow, a teaching about "fullness" would be appropriate here, but I do not wish to write a whole treatise on the banquet hall. Building up the spiritual body is an important factor in the health of the Bride. John's third epistle tells us, "I wish above all things that thou mayest prosper and be in health even as thy soul prospereth." Sometimes, it is of interest to look over a congregation and imagine how they might look if reversed!

ADDENDUM 2

FURTHER THOUGHTS

Random thoughts gleaned, while walking through the Song, are concepts not included in the general text for one reason or another, but they do present some challenging areas for consideration. Review them, and perhaps some point of reference will be gained for having done so. They are disjoined, so you will only have scattered thoughts presented.

1. Many of the love passages in the Bible are in conjunction with other attributes. Sometimes "love" is the first attribute; sometimes, it is the last. Why? Could it be we are given a hint in the Greek word *Agapao* which begins with Alpha and ends with Omega? This is an encompassing word. This kind of love penetrates every situation involving the believer; it is the beginning of every consideration and the end of all considerations. This is why it starts in Genesis, and it ends in Revelation. It encompasses the Pauline doctrine of I Corinthians 13 and the doctrine of Peter in II Peter 1:5-7. Love becomes the golden thread woven at first in God's dealing with man and used to bind the heart of His Son to His Bride.

2. Brides are people. They are people who got carried away in their love. Do brides who fall in love with Jesus ever say, like some earthly brides, "I wish I had never met him?" Jesus locked out a few who thought they were brides.

3. How is it everything I learned in psychology and sociology about the needs of man are met by Jesus in His love dealings with the Shulamite. He missed nothing I can find. He included security, new experiences, worthiness, etc.; yes, I believe He included everything. Is this why He is altogether lovely?

4. Awkwardness occurs in love relationships; isn't it all right to be awkward in our relationship to Jesus?

5. In order to be a bride, we have to know something about Him the rest of the world doesn't know. Some things I know that the unbeliever doesn't know:

He has a special place in the kingdom
He is willing to share it
He is never selfish
He spares no expense for our comfort
He wants to share in intimacy
He shares His dreams, mission,

desires in those intimate times He listens
There are just too many things I know to write them,
but I could.

6. Yield, Yield, Yield as He entreats; yield as the first response. He gives time for us to reflect after our yielding, but yielding is the basis for our interaction.

7. Abundance is a part of the blessing of His love. He can't love without giving. Be greedy when it comes to taking from God. "And the tribe of Benjamin took too much." We have to change our attitude toward the kingdom. Vast wealth is not depleted by a constant drain.

8. Brides change their views of the "beloved" the further they go with him. They possess more of him. They learn to anticipate him. Can we get to where we anticipate Jesus' moves? O yes.

9. The atmosphere changes with Jesus. He always speaks of birds singing, freedom to skip along the hills, to be carefree, even to stop to smell the flowers.

10. Random thoughts on being a bride:

You have to want to be one to be one
You know it's going to get intimate
You have to learn his ways and live by his ways
You find out what is yours
You get to really know yourself

11. The words "glad" and "rejoice" reoccur frequently. There is an exhilarating attitude the closer we get to Him. No grumps know Him.

12. A poem written while contemplating the oneness of Jesus and His bride.

Now flows the love between them,
Born in Heaven's plan,
Where kingly breast beats as One
With fairest daughter of Man
Embracing her, such rapturous climb
Their person lost in their entwine,
Each hailing other's virtuous hue,
A pledge that God would not eschew,
For they, once two, are ONE.